from a house to a home

from a house to a home

simple ideas and projects to enrich everyday family life

Jemima Mills

COLLINS & BROWN

To my husband, Titus,
and
to my parents, John and Kate Dyson,
with unending love and gratitude

First published in Great Britain in 2000
by Collins & Brown Limited
London House
Great Eastern Wharf
Parkgate Road
London SW11 4NQ

Distributed in the United States and Canada by Sterling Publishing Co.
387 Park Avenue South, New York, NY 10016 USA

1 3 5 7 9 8 6 4 2

British Library Cataloguing-in-Publication Data:
A catalogue record for this book is available from the British Library.

ISBN 1 85585 800 2

Conceived, edited and designed by Collins & Brown Limited

Editor: Gillian Haslam
Copy Editor: Alison Wormleighton
Designer: Christine Wood
Photographer: Jacqui Hurst

Reproduction by Global Colour, Malaysia
Printed and bound by Dai Nippon Printing Co (Hong Kong) Ltd

This book was typeset using Neue Helvetica Thin and Fineprint.

Contents

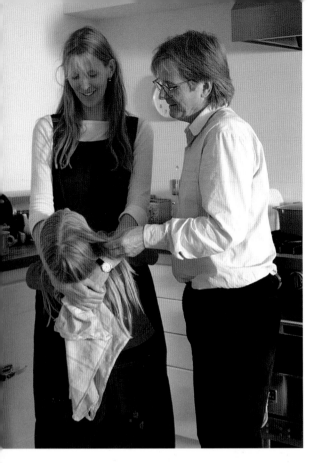

Introduction

It fills me with great joy to be part of a warm and supportive family. My memories of family life are intensely vivid. I treasure my childhood and teenage memories and look back on a lot of happy everyday moments: my dad walking me to school testing me on my times tables; sitting on my mother's lap while she read *Elmer The Elephant* for the hundredth time; putting on 'punk rock shows' with my brothers and sisters. I remember the laughter, the joy and the intimacy.

But my family life has never been plain sailing and I have certainly had my fair share of tears. There have been the battles and the bickering between my brothers and sisters, like the time I was so cross with my brother that I poured a bottle of milk on his head. There have been the disasters, the sorrows and quite a bit of slamming of doors. A family can contain the people we love most in the world but find the hardest to get on with. When growing up in a family you cannot choose the people you live with, but learning to get on with them is a vital lesson in life.

The reality of family life is that it is a mixture of good times and bad. I look back and realize that all my family memories are fond ones because they were born out of a shared experience. If there is one word that describes family, it is sharing. Family is the coming together of people, sharing their home and their lives. Togetherness is the essence of family life.

Bedtime, bathtime and mealtimes are some of the everyday humdrum routines around which family life revolves. Such routines are the foundation upon which the interaction of family life is built. They can be joyful times, or difficult and frustrating – but it is the sharing of them that family living is all

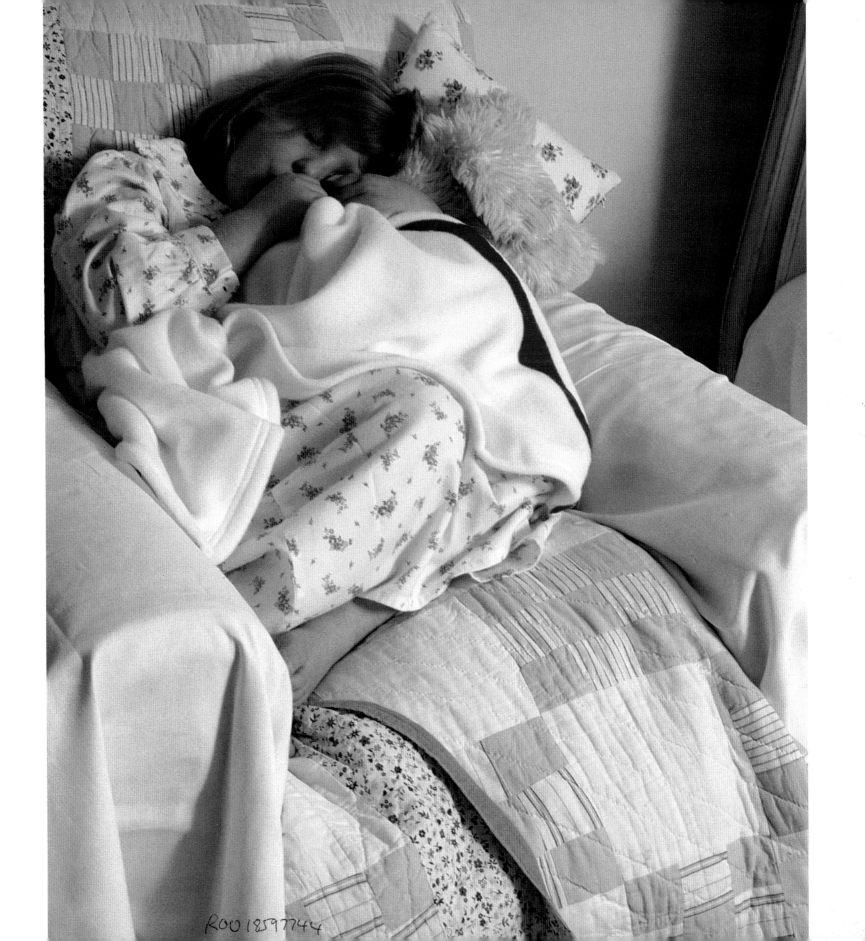

about. This book is a celebration of everyday family life. It captures the daily routines of households and puts the environment in which these routines take place, the family home, in the spotlight.

The images in this book portray family life in idyllic circumstances; the sun is shining, the children are smiling and the cushions are always plumped up. What the photographs do not show are the toys pushed under the bed at the last minute, the yogurt spilt all over the floor and the sofa covered in dog hair and sweet wrappers. There is no such thing as a perfect happy family. But the images do not dwell on the difficult and awkward times of family life, even though these are an integral part of any living family. Instead, the images are designed to inspire.

This book strives to reclaim and to celebrate family spirit, in which adults and children come together to enjoy simple activities and pleasures. Whatever type of family you live in – whether you have one child, no children, fourteen children or a hamster – this book is about feeling good about family. My prayer is that young and old can dip into this book and get excited about family life. The family home and the everyday routines within it can be looked at afresh and celebrated for all they signify to the life of a family. Happy family memories are founded on a lot of ordinary moments. Sharing these moments is what helps to bind a family together – so take some time out and enjoy being together.

Jemima Mills

Family Home

A safe, comfortable haven, the home is where parent and child alike can retreat from the outside world and recharge their batteries. It provides the reassuringly familiar surroundings in which the daily routines of family life take place – somewhere that everyone in the family can work, rest and play.

A family home is a place where everyone who crosses the threshold – both family and friends – should feel both welcomed and relaxed. Perfect tidiness is not always conducive to relaxation; a bit of chaos and signs of real life are what makes a house into a home.

Kitchen style 16

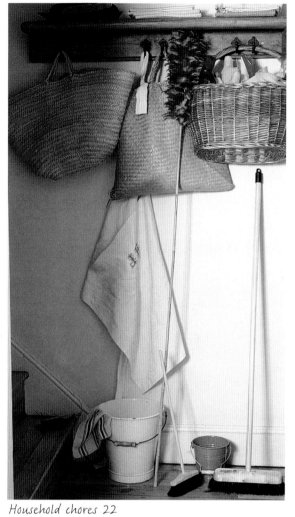

Household chores 22

Family rooms 24

Family gallery 33

Poorly bed 36

Home office 40

Bedtime 45

Parents' bedrooms 62

Bathtime 67

Time to soak 73

Friends to stay 76

Outdoor living 78

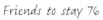

The words family and home often go together. As the main setting for family life, a family home is constantly evolving with the ever-changing needs of its various occupants. It is a place of both laughter and tears – somewhere to work and to play; to share the everyday humdrum routines and to celebrate special days and events; to be alone and to be together. A place of emotional warmth and physical comfort, a family home is not just a shelter but a real sanctuary from the world outside. An easy, lived-in, informal home will make for a welcoming home.

Creating a family home involves putting together an attractive space that everyone can grow to love, as well as a functional one that can easily encompass the daily life of each family member. It requires creating an atmosphere of comfort and relaxation and a welcoming environment. Of course, the home can also be full of frustrations: nothing is tidy for long, everything needs mending, the household chores grow by the day. Often the requirements are temporarily conflicting or mutually exclusive – in providing somewhere in which the family can come together, for example, it may sometimes be impossible for individuals to be alone when they want to be. A parent may find that they are treading the fine line between giving children space to be themselves yet having to ensure that they also put their toys away.

Every family home has its own unique character, reflecting the personality, needs and interests of the family that lives within its walls. This book, and in particular this chapter, celebrates family homes that reflect the spirit of family life. Explore the chapter for inspiring ideas, useful hints and practical projects for turning a house or apartment into a family home. Be inspired by the ideas and imbue them with your own individuality, wit and style.

Kitchen style

A family kitchen is often a delightful expression of the character of a family. It may be crammed with children's drawings, postcards, family china perhaps passed through the generations, toys scattered on the floor, notes reminding people to do things and a sense of organized chaos. Or it may be a place only for preparing food – a highly polished, spotlessly clean environment where toys are not allowed and clutter is hidden away. Whatever its style, a kitchen is likely to reveal quite a bit about the personality of the owners.

The kitchen is generally the heart of today's home. Not only is it the venue for mealtimes, where members of the family come together to eat, but it's also a place where friends gather. The table tends to be the focus of the kitchen, as it is a place not just to eat, but to prepare food, have a cup of

Far left: French doors giving access to the garden guarantee that the kitchen will be central to family life.

Near left (top): Practicality and a warm welcome combine in the kitchen, particularly when it benefits from the permanent warmth of an Aga.

Near left (centre and bottom) and below: Shelf edgings, curtains inside wire cupboard doors and tablecloths are all ways to use fabric in a kitchen.

Below right: A kitchen dresser allows everyday china to be both ready to hand and on display. Plates decorated by the children are given pride of place.

coffee or spread out the morning newspaper, and for children to help with cooking, do homework, play games or do craft work.

The first requirement of any kitchen is for it to be highly practical, providing space for a plethora of large and small appliances as well as plenty of storage for everything from peppercorns to a complete dinner service. Easy-to-use shelving and cupboards that fit everything in and make items accessible are essential, otherwise a kitchen soon begins to burst at the seams.

Because a family will spend a lot of time in the kitchen, it needs to be not only functional but attractive, welcoming and comfortable too. It is a room where decorating can be fun. Paint the cabinets in strong colours or line glass doors with fabric, edge the shelves in colourful waxed or plasticized fabrics so they are easy to clean and introduce lively patterns with curtains, cushions or tablecloths.

Kitchen safety

Young children tend to regard the kitchen as their personal playground, but it is unfortunately the most hazardous room in the home. However, making the kitchen safe for children is fairly straightforward if you follow these tips:

❥ If you have to carry a hot dish or a pan of boiling water across a large space, you are more likely to trip on a child. Therefore, the hob (cooktop), oven and sink need to be relatively close together. By the same token, they shouldn't be sited near a door, as children rushing into the kitchen won't be looking where they are going. If your kitchen does have these layout problems and you are unable to rearrange it, keep children away from the hob and oven when you are using either of them.

❥ Creating a play area at the other end of the room, still within eyeshot but away from the food preparation and cooking area, will help prevent children and their toys from becoming a hazard.

❥ When pans are on the hob, ensure that the handles are not overhanging, otherwise a child could grab them. It's also a good idea to fit a guard rail on the hob until children are old enough not to reach for handles.

❥ Drawers should have safety stops so that children cannot pull an entire drawer down on their heads.

❥ Keep drawers and cupboards shut to avoid banged heads as toddlers race around. Fit childproof catches on any drawers and cupboards whose contents pose a risk. If toddlers want to empty a cupboard, the pan cupboard is probably safe, or give them a pot of wooden spoons to empty.

❥ Keep sharp things, breakables, cleaning materials and other harmful items out of a young child's reach. Even the most innocuous items, like ceramic baking beans, are a hazard in babies' and toddlers' hands (and mouths).

❥ Always place knives point down in a dishwasher or when draining.

❥ Don't store heavy or breakable items on unstable racks or small tables that a child could pull over.

❥ If children need to stand on something to reach the worktop when helping you, a chair or special set of steps is safer than a stool.

❥ Make it clear which is the hot tap – perhaps tie some red string around it.

❥ Never leave trailing electrical leads, which children could yank or trip over.

❥ Include in the kitchen a low, deep drawer or a chest in which children can keep toys, to make them less likely to leave their things scattered around the floor where people could trip over them.

❥ Make sure that the floor surface is non-slip and easy to clean.

Left: *Children quickly find ways, however precarious, of reaching things that are at grown-up height. This is certainly a good way to develop balancing skills but make sure the child knows that they can only play like this when an adult is present – standing on a chair may be safer.*

Right: *Siting the cooker near the sink prevents you from having to walk a long way carrying a pan of boiling water while children are underfoot. Worktop on either side of the cooker provides a safe parking place for pans, particularly if it includes a heat-resistant surface.*

Above: *The steel staircase makes an ideal surface for magnets, a place to store important memos as well as a good opportunity for a child to learn the alphabet.*

The modern kitchen

Sleek, modern homes and minimalist style are well suited to the seriously functional kitchen, designed for families who are keen cooks and dedicated food connoisseurs. High-performance appliances, purpose-built storage and uncluttered surfaces ensure that the kitchen is highly practical. Although an absence of clutter may seem anathema to the average family, the minimal effort and maximum efficiency deriving from such a kitchen have to be good news for any exhausted parent. And if the room does start to look too clinical, a few choice pieces of children's art, carefully placed, will look stunning against this pristine background.

For a family-oriented kitchen of this kind, in which daily life is centred around the kitchen, a large table or a long, wide run of worktop on which the family can prepare food, eat, read, work, draw, entertain and even conduct business meetings is ideal. The surface is very quickly cleared and wiped after each use, ready for the next activity. Storage space can be designed so that not only cooking equipment and tableware but also most appliances are out of the way, and everything that is needed to prepare a meal is within reach. Furniture, apart from seating, can thus be kept to a minimum. Apart from anything else, it means that riding around the kitchen on a bike becomes so much easier for the children!

Right: *With so many activities taking place in the kitchen, a powerful extractor fan that will scoop up the steam and smells from cooking is essential.*

Far right: *Tailor-made storage with shelves to accommodate the exact height of glasses is very easy to achieve and makes efficient use of space.*

Right: *A long work surface with an overhang allows people to sit at it on bar stools, which slide neatly underneath when not in use. A special, higher stool means a small child will be seated at the right height and will feel as important as everyone else.*

'Cleaning your house while your kids are still growing is like shoveling the walk before it stops snowing.'

Phyllis Diller

Household chores

With all the comings and goings of family life, tidying, cleaning, and doing the laundry and the dishes can seem like never-ending tasks. It's helpful to forge out a routine for household chores. Every household will have different requirements, according to its lifestyle. The kitchen and bathrooms will probably require cleaning daily, while other rooms will need it only about once a week, so you could clean them on different days. Put a few hours aside once a week for a big clean – perhaps on Saturday morning or some other time when all the family are around to help.

Teach all family members to do their own share of the work automatically. If you have a dishwasher, encourage everyone to load their own dishes into it after a meal and to unload the clean dishes whenever it needs to be done. Wastepaper baskets and the kitchen rubbish bin should be emptied as necessary by whoever happens to be using them.

Similarly, children should make their own beds and be encouraged to keep their bedrooms tidy. This particular task can be an ongoing battle so you need to lay down basic rules. It is up to you to set your own standard of tidiness, but to expect perfect tidiness every day is probably unrealistic. A compromise could be that children make their beds each morning and then tidy up on Saturday. If the room is in such chaos that they are completely overwhelmed by it, you could suggest that they make a start and then you will come and help. Or perhaps, for young children, put the toys in a big pile for them first and they can put them in the basket. Turn tidying into a game, such as a race to see who can be the first to put ten toys into the basket. Get hold of a stopwatch and time them tidying up, or put on some silly 'tidying up' music.

Children are perfectly able to help and can learn to do everything eventually. Sweeping, dusting, washing up and drying dishes are all easy household chores for a child to start with. Older children can do more difficult tasks like vacuuming and the laundry. Don't bully them into doing a task – you shouldn't let them get away with doing nothing but they need to be taught to volunteer for it. Be realistic about their abilities, however, and avoid overwhelming them with jobs. You could allocate, say, one hour on Saturday mornings for the children's chores. A rota system will help prevent a child feeling hard done by when they get the worst job.

Delegating is a sign of trust. Children may need to be shown how to do a chore but then they should be left to do some of it on their own, even if you

Top left: *If you do not want to overcrowd a kitchen or a bathroom with laundry, build a simple cupboard for the laundry appliances. Hang laundry bags on the inside of the door. When the laundry becomes overwhelming or instant tidying is necessary, you can simply close the door.*

Centre left: *Stack the clean laundry in a basket and encourage the children to sort it out in piles and put it away.*

Bottom left: *A child-sized dustpan and brush may make sweeping into a game rather than a chore.*

Far left: *Miniature versions of cleaning implements, such as brooms and buckets, will allow children to work alongside adults and copy the techniques.*

Below: *An alternative way to store clothes is to make labels showing the shapes of clothes for the fronts of storage boxes and baskets. A child can easily grab an outfit, and it might encourage simple and quick putting away of clean laundry too.*

Right: *Make the most of good weather to dry clothes and bed linen outside. Children love helping to hang things on the line.*

will have to redo it all later. Instigate a reward system for a job well done – stickers or smiley faces are ideal for younger children. Helping with chores can also be a way for youngsters to earn extra pocket money. Make a list of jobs for the school holidays. Each job can have its payment beside it and the children can choose which tasks they want to do. Don't pay for a job that is only half-done, but do help them finish it if necessary. And try to avoid being forced to pay for everything – it's important for children to learn the joy of doing things for other people and the satisfaction of completing a task. Encourage them with lots of genuine praise. This will help ensure that they are willing helpers next time. Children enjoy helping, not only because they thrive on praise but also because it makes them feel grown-up and responsible. It's up to adults to make the task fun!

'There are three ways to get something done: do it yourself, hire someone, or forbid your kids to do it.'

Monta Crane

Family rooms

To relax in real comfort, the room that is variously called a living room, sitting room or family room is where most people gather. In the old days, a home might have a 'company' living room which no one was allowed to mess up, and another room, often called a family room, where the family could relax. These days, guests tend to be treated informally and are encouraged to join the family in the kitchen and the family living area. Thus, whatever it is called, the living area in today's home is in essence a family room.

A comfortable family room welcomes you home. To sink into a familiar armchair after a long day at work or school is a real sign of being home. This is where you can relax, unwind and chat in complete ease after a busy day.

In many homes the living (and also dining) rooms that were once reserved for company have had their walls knocked down to create one large living space for all the family to be together. Sometimes it is open-plan with the kitchen; perhaps one end will be dedicated to cooking and eating, and the other will have a comfortable chair and sofa.

Whatever the arrangement, this is a room for comfort and relaxation. The challenge is to accommodate the different needs of all the members of the household. Everyone will probably watch television or listen to music in the family room. In addition, parents will want to relax there together when the children are in bed, and also to entertain friends sometimes. In the daytime a parent may have a desk in the family room, so that it also serves as a home office. And the children's toys, games and activities will almost certainly spill into the room. Much as children love to be underfoot when a parent is working in the kitchen, the family room's soft sofas and rugs or carpet are irresistible to children, who will enjoy jumping and sprawling on them.

If there is enough space, it may be possible to give the children their own living area. This can serve as a playroom when they are young and a den when they become teenagers. It doesn't have to be a big space – a spare room, landing or corner of the kitchen may be ideal. A playroom can be a strictly children-only zone, or it can include one or two comfortable chairs for adults, too. Toys, games and books can all be stored in this room. It might be fun to create a reading corner with small chairs to sit on and bookshelves at child height. This can also be a good room for a homework desk and a computer, particularly if a child's bedroom is small. (For more about furnishing a playroom, see page 118.) When children approach the teenage years, bring in a comfortable sofa-bed and big squashy floor cushions, a television

Above: *Children love 'grown-up' treats, perhaps a drink downstairs before bedtime, wrapped in dressing gowns by the fire. They will particularly enjoy this if the parents are entertaining friends as they will feel more included in the party.*

Right: *Try not to make the television the focal point of the room, as it can easily become the focus of family life, too. Choose a set that is small, or put it in a cupboard where it can be hidden behind a door when not in use. This television stand was made from an old trolley found in a junk shop and painted a bright colour. The television can simply be wheeled out when a favourite programme is on and put away afterwards.*

and a stereo system. Teenagers love to loll around and will welcome a private room to retreat to where they can listen to music with their friends. It is also a good room for sleep-overs, particularly if it is well out of earshot of the rest of the family's bedrooms.

While children are young, a few safety precautions should be taken in any living areas to avoid accidents:

❥ Make sure that electric flexes are hidden away, and are not in a place where they can be pulled or tripped over.

❥ If rugs are slippery, put non-slip mats underneath them.

❥ Breakable objects should be placed out of a child's reach.

❥ Children love an empty space to play in, so take the coffee table away until they are older. You should certainly avoid a glass table.

❥ It may be an idea to hide the video or stereo, to avoid pieces of toast or building bricks being posted through the flap.

❥ Patio doors and French windows are a hazard. Put some protective film over them to stop a child from being injured running through them.

❥ Make sure that the television or any other heavy object cannot be pulled over by children on top of themselves.

In any home with children, the family room will undergo a lot of wear and tear. Sofa cushions and throws will regularly be pulled onto the floor, jumped on and turned into dens. Sticky fingers, felt-tipped pens, spilt juice and crumbs will be impossible to avoid. Animal hair from family cats or dogs gets everywhere. Children and animals are not the only culprits – the odd red wine spill is also familiar in most households. Do not, therefore, harbour any expectations of a well-used family room being spotless and smart.

There are, however, ways to limit the damage. Rather than fitted upholstery, choose slip covers for sofas and armchairs, as they can be taken off and cleaned. Choose colours and patterns that do not easily show the dirt. If you have always dreamed of a white sofa, wait until the children are older, or cover it with a throw that can easily be washed. At any rate, scattering throws and cushions over seating makes it more welcoming and relaxing. When they are made from exotic fabrics or colourful blankets, they add colour, pattern, texture and an individual personal quality to a room. And if you get tired of the designs, they are easier to replace than the entire sofa.

Cover a wall with bookshelves, hang your favourite pictures, and light candles in the evening (out of the reach of youngsters) to make a really welcoming atmosphere. In the daytime, place a chair by a window to enjoy a peaceful moment soaking up the sunlight.

'That house was a perfect house, whether you like food or sleep, or storytelling, or singing, or just sitting and thinking best, or a pleasant mixture of them all. Merely to be there was a cure for weariness, fear and sadness.'

J R R Tolkien

Left: *Put a comfortable chair in the kitchen – you'll find it's ideal for grabbing a few moments of relaxation in the middle of the day or while waiting for food to cook. It also makes the kitchen a sociable room and a pleasant place to chat to others while cooking.*

Right: *Comfort is conducive to relaxation, so make easy chairs a priority. Cover them in favourite colours or patterns, bringing in accent colours with contrast piping and eclectic cushions. Loose covers are ideal because they can be taken off and washed when they are covered in sticky finger marks.*

Cosy living

Despite central heating and double glazing, the seasons – thankfully – still penetrate into our homes and well-insulated lives. In the summer, windows are thrown open, and the garden or park becomes a place to play, rest and enjoy alfresco meals or picnics. In the winter, however, our instincts are to hibernate, to snuggle by a warm fire or relax on a pile of warm cushions and shut ourselves off from the elements.

It takes little effort to make a family room cosy for the winter. Cover the soft furniture with warm blankets or soft throws. Warm up the colours of a room by adding some cushions in rich berry colours. Change the textures of the fabrics, from cottons and linens to deep velvets and thickly woven jacquards or wool. Bare floorboards can be cold so put warm rugs on the floor. For instant 'winter-weight' curtains, attach lightweight blankets to curtain poles with café clips.

Even in centrally heated homes, an open fire is lovely, creating an atmosphere of relaxation and contemplation. Watching the dancing flames of a log fire can be mesmerizing. If you do not have an open fire, light candles and dot them around the room to create the same atmosphere of flickering flames. Place a group of candles together in an unused fireplace to give the illusion of a fire. (Remember never to leave burning candles unattended.)

Creating a cosy, inviting atmosphere in a room will naturally draw the family together. Devise winter treats to make the season as exciting as summer. Play special games, toast marshmallows or make delicious warming drinks.

'When it snows, she has no fear for her household, for all of them are clothed in scarlet.'

Proverbs

extra-special hot chocolate

1 medium-sized bar of plain chocolate
550ml (1 pint) milk
2 drops vanilla essence

❥ Slowly melt the chocolate in a heatproof bowl over a pan of boiling water.
❥ Warm the milk. Very gradually add the milk and vanilla essence to the chocolate, stirring all the time so it does not go lumpy.
❥ Pour into mugs to serve.

Far right: *In the winter, blankets used as throws add instant cosiness to a room,*

Right: *An open fire is an effective way to dry clothes after a wet, wintry walk. If children are about, use a childproof guard in front of a fire. Keep lit candles (and matches or lighters) out of children's reach.*

Minimal living

With clever design and plenty of ingenious storage ideas, a family home can be still a clean, simple and clutter-free space. A minimal style of interior design provides not only a welcome sense of space and light but also a highly functional living area that will easily accommodate the various needs of the entire family. Whether in a city loft, a warehouse conversion, a studio apartment or a house, a minimal style of decoration creates a calm, unfussy environment in which everyone can relax after a strenuous, demanding day. The sheer absence of everyday domestic clutter also allows it to double up as an ideal working environment, whether to hold business meetings or to spread out children's homework. This sort of home can also be far easier and quicker to keep clean!

The spacious, open-plan living areas associated with minimalism are, of course, great for children to play in. They can set out elaborate games on the wide floors, build an indoor den or ride small bikes or trucks around the room. What's more, they can run around the home and burn off excess energy without having to weave through a multitude of doorways or between pieces of furniture.

Left: *Design storage so that toys are quick to tidy away, allowing adults to enjoy the space for themselves in the evenings.*

Right: *The wall by the staircase is given over completely to bookshelves. The books on the top shelf can be reached by climbing the stairs.*

Below: *A large, uncluttered floor area is ideal for children to play on and set up games.*

Right: *Professional family portraits collected over the years will be enjoyed when they are new and will be treasured for generations to come. The children could do their own family portraits and these could be framed, too.*

Below: *Frame a collection of black-and-white family photographs that encompass different generations. Black-and-white photographs always have a timeless appeal, and old and new pictures will hang together effectively. Choose simple, unfussy frames that will not detract from the images.*

Family gallery

Photographs are revealing expressions of the character of a family. Not only do they capture happy memories on film to treasure always, but they become an evocative record of family history. When a child grows up and starts a family of their own, the photos will give their offspring an instantaneous image of their parent's childhood. Photographs also become important reminders of relatives who have passed away and of significant events like weddings or special anniversaries.

Many of the best family photographs are snapshots, and these often look more effective displayed as a collage of images. This provides an ideal way to remember a significant event like a party or holiday. Place all the images together in a frame with none of the background showing, and cut some of the images up into different shapes. You could include other memorabilia as well – for example, a collage of a holiday by the sea might include seashells decorating the frame. Snapshots also work well in smaller individual frames which are easily displayed in groups on mantelpieces or shelves.

Rather than scattering family photos all over the main rooms, find a specific wall in the home to turn into a 'gallery' where you can hang them all together. A hallway or staircase wall is ideal, because it is usually the largest empty expanse of wall, and all the family can glance at the photos as they pass through the home. You could unify the display by restricting it to particular types of photos: perhaps a collection of school photos of the children over the years, or old black-and-white or sepia photos going back generations.

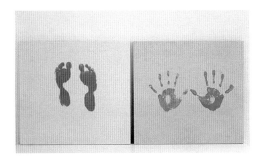

framed handprints

For an alternative to a height chart, print footprints or handprints onto squares of painted wood. Start when children are tiny and do a new one every few years (write the date on the back). This can be a messy business, so put plenty on newspaper on the floor or work surface first, and make sure there is a basin nearby so paint can quickly be washed off. Framed hand- and footprints also make great presents, especially for grandparents who may not see their grandchildren regularly.

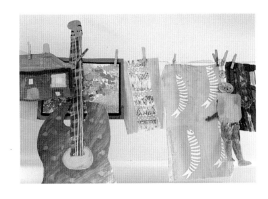

Far left and left: Displaying art can be as simple as running some string across a room and creating a washing line of artwork hanging up with clothes pegs.

As an alternative to photographs, create an 'art' gallery by covering the wall with pictures. You certainly don't need lots of smart paintings to create a visual feast on the walls. Children's paintings and drawings look wonderful, and with simple frames around them they enter a different league. In addition, you could frame hand-made cards, a poem, a child's first story or flowers and leaves that children have pressed. Not only will youngsters be thrilled to see their work in such a place of honour, but they will be eager to produce more. For extra interest, you could add other relevant items to the display, such as framed children's illustrations, prints, picture postcards or posters. Or simply hunt for quirky old pictures in flea markets and transform them by changing the frames.

Frames can vary from simple, inexpensive wooden or clip versions to more elaborate decorative frames. Old, slightly battered frames have a lot of character and can still be found in flea markets and antique shops (though it is increasingly difficult to find real bargains). You can make a collection of varied pictures and photographs cohesive by framing them all in a similar way or in matching frames, but a colourful hotchpotch of varied pictures has charm, too. Adding a suitable mount around a picture can sometimes completely transform it, giving it more importance, changing the proportions and possibly even improving the colour balance.

The way you arrange the pictures obviously depends on how many you are hanging, their size, the space available and your own personal tastes. In particular, if they are running up the wall of a stairway, the arrangement is more or less dictated by the diagonal line of the stairs. In other situations, there are various 'classic' layouts that could be used as a basis for the arrangement. For example, the pictures can all appear to hang from, or to stand on, an imaginary horizontal line, or they can be arranged on one side or the other of an imaginary vertical line. Sometimes it works well for the outside edges of the outermost frames in a group to form a rectangle, a square or a triangle. Whatever arrangement you choose, be sure to try it out on the floor first.

As an alternative to hanging pictures on the wall, you could display them on a narrow wooden shelf running along the wall at chair-rail height; a small lip on the shelf will stop them from sliding off. However, if there are young children in the family, frames without glass will be safest, as youngsters will undoubtedly want to try their hand at re-arranging the pictures themselves (and, quite naturally, putting their own handiwork or portraits in the most prominent places).

Above: *Photographs and pictures can look effective just propped up on a shelf, a casual style of display that suits an informal home.*

Right: *An ever-changing display of photographs stuck on a fridge door with magnets or on a noticeboard with pins has an irresistible charm. This type of 'rogues' gallery' also helps young children to recognize and form bonds with friends and family they may not see very often.*

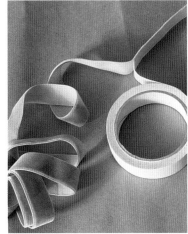

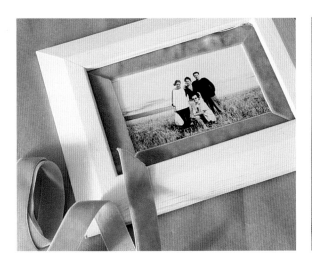

velvet ribbon mounts

Photographs look more finished if they have a mount of some sort around them, and velvet ribbon is an attractive hand-made alternative to a cardboard mount.

❥ *Choose wooden frames that are the appropriate size for your photographs – ideally, each inside dimension should equal the width or length of the photo plus twice the width of the velvet ribbon. Take the glass out and paint the frames in emulsion (latex) paint so that they all match. When dry, apply a coat of flat acrylic varnish over the top. Leave to dry, then replace the glass.*

❥ *Stick double-sided sticking tape along the back of a strip of velvet ribbon. This will ensure that the edges can be cut cleanly and the ribbon will lie flat on the photograph.*

❥ *Cut the ribbon into four strips corresponding to the inside dimensions of the frame, and mitring the corners. Trim off any sticking tape that is wider than the ribbon.*

❥ *Centre the photo on the backing, then stick the strips of ribbon neatly around the edges. Now place the photo with its mount in the frame.*

Poorly bed

Illness is a familiar feature of family life. Not only are there the usual childhood ailments such as chickenpox, but everyday colds, coughs and flu are also regrettably common, especially in winter.

As well as plenty of rest, lots of liquid and possibly some medicine, a sick child needs a great deal of loving care and attention. Because the child may quickly get bored or lonely if left in the bedroom for too long, it is sometimes a good idea to make up a sofa as a bed, so that the child can be near other people during the day. If the television is in the same room, this will enable the child to watch it in comfort. Watching a video is an ideal activity for a sick child because it is so passive – with a pounding headache, even reading can seem like hard work. Lay the sofa out with plenty of pillows, a duvet and an extra blanket so that the child can feel really cosy and cosseted. (You may also wish to put some towels down on the sofa first, to protect it.)

Place a table near the bed and put on it a special drink container which you keep topping up. Try using a curly-whirly straw, a special cup or anything that will encourage the child to drink. If the parent nursing the child has work to do elsewhere in the house, it may be an idea to put a bell by the bed so the child can ring it if they need help or are about to be sick.

Try to find special treats for the invalid. Fill a box with books, quiet games and special treats, such as stickers, felt pens, a new comic or soft toys. It can be known as the 'poorly box' and only sick children are allowed to play with the treasures inside.

Below left: *Always cover a hot water bottle with something before giving it to a child. This cover was hand-made from soft fleece fabric, which makes it comforting to cuddle.*

Below right: *Make a 'poorly box' filled with treasures to be discovered only by a child who is not well.*

Far right: *A child may feel lonely in the bedroom during the day so make a bed up on a sofa, with a special 'poorly quilt' and a favourite bear. Place within reach a drink to sip regularly and a bell to ring if they need help.*

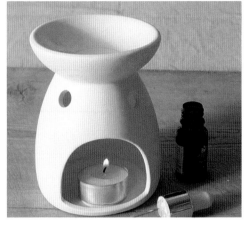

Remedies

For common ailments like colds and flu, for which there is no real treatment and which have to take their course, simple household remedies can be used to help relieve discomfort until children are well again. When children are ill, you don't have to make them wrap up warm, stay in bed and eat invalid food – instead, you should just take your cue from them. If they don't want to lie down, that's fine. In fact, staying in bed can sometimes even prolong an illness if it makes the child more listless or prevents them from getting a proper sleep at night. And when they do need the rest, their bodies will naturally tell them to lie down or at least rest in an armchair. A normal room temperature and fresh air are fine; feverish children are actually more at risk from getting too hot. And if they don't feel like eating, don't worry – it won't hurt them, so long as they get plenty of fluids.

Feeling sick and vomiting can be very distressing for children. If they have been sick a lot, there is a risk of becoming dehydrated, so every 10–15 minutes or so give them small drinks, especially cold water with a pinch of salt and a teaspoon of glucose or sugar added. Flat lemonade or cola is good for an upset tummy, too, as it helps to settle it and provide some energy. Dilute fruit juices, and don't offer milk. When children regain their appetite, start them on something that isn't too rich.

When a child (or an adult) has a blocked nose, a vaporizer is a good decongestant and, if used with a few drops of essential eucalyptus oil, will help clear the nasal passages.

Above left: For colds, blocked noses and sinuses, put some drops of eucalyptus oil in the top of a vaporizer set over a night light. The heat will release the eucalyptus vapours into the air, which should then be breathed deeply. Alternatively, add a few drops of oil to a basin of hot water and sit with a towel draped over your head..

Centre left: Ginger and lemon drink can be enjoyed when someone is either healthy or ill. It is very cleansing, helping to dispel toxins. Chop up pieces of root ginger and put them in a mug of hot water with a slice of lemon. The ginger is good for the immune system, and lemon juice is full of vitamin C.

Bottom left: Lemon and honey drink is very soothing for a bad cold. Squeeze the juice from a lemon into a mug of hot water and stir in a spoonful of honey. For an adult, make it into a hot toddy by adding a dash of whisky. Drink at bedtime to aid sleep.

Most children's medicines now have a nice taste, but sometimes it can be difficult to get youngsters to take pills, in which case you can crush the pills and hide them in a spoonful of honey or jam. If you remind children that their medicine will make them better, and if you act as though you don't expect them to object, there is a good chance that they will take it quite happily.

When children have bad sore throats, plain lemon ice lollies are ideal. The lollies cool them down a little if they have a temperature and are soothing on the throat. If necessary, call on doctor Teddy to bring in refreshments and cheer them up.

The medicine cabinet

Keep a well-stocked medicine cabinet in case of emergencies. Remember that it should be out of reach of children and locked. The basics might be:

- ❥ antiseptic lotion, assorted adhesive plasters (Band-Aids) and bandages
- ❥ gauze dressings (for dressing wounds, cleaning grazes and getting grit out of eyes)
- ❥ adhesive strapping (for holding a dressing in place)
- ❥ junior-strength and adult-strength painkillers such as paracetamol (or aspirin for children over 12 and adults)
- ❥ sting-relieving cream or spray
- ❥ cough syrup
- ❥ tweezers and scissors
- ❥ a clinical thermometer

Below left: Garlic and honey: raw garlic is very good for soothing a cold, so peel and chop some cloves of garlic and mix them with honey. Eating garlic raw is much easier this way.

Below : Blackcurrant drink: dissolve a large spoon of blackcurrant jam in a mug of hot water. This makes a warm and soothing drink for a sore throat and also contains useful vitamin C.

Right: Give a child a favourite blanket and a cuddly teddy bear to snuggle to make them feel better.

'A family is a unit composed not only of children, but of men, women, an occasional animal, and the common cold.'

Ogden Nash

'If you find honey, eat just enough.'

Proverbs

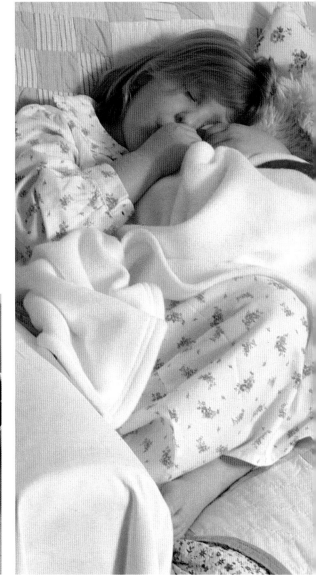

Home office

With the boom in telecommunications and growing use of the Internet, it is becoming increasingly popular and easy to work from home. And even if paid work mainly takes place out of the home, running a family itself involves a lot of paperwork. Transforming a corner of the home, if not a whole room, into a home office will therefore be an enormous boon.

An office area can take up a small space, especially if storage is carefully designed. All you have to find room for are a table or desk, a chair, some filing arrangements and a lamp. A landing or hall that is big enough may be ideal, with shelving under the stairs. Or you could simply put a desk at one end of the living room, dining room or guest bedroom. (Try to keep work out of the master bedroom so that it can be reserved as a room to rest in.)

If someone in your family does paid work at home on a full-time basis, a more sophisticated office will be necessary. The beauty of a home office is that you can have the best of both worlds: an environment that combines domestic home comforts with the efficiency of a 'real' office. Achieving this, however, may require considerable ingenuity and planning.

You will probably need to find room for quite a bit of storage as well as a fax machine, computer and printer, a desk and a comfortable chair, any specialist equipment, plus enough work surface to be able to spread out paperwork. Good lighting and heating are essential if a lot of time will be spent in the office. Finally, you will almost certainly need extra power points.

Left and right: The living room is often an ideal spot for a desk, as it is less likely to be disturbed than if it were in the kitchen. If there are no drawers in the desk, use boxes that stack, painting them to match your scheme. Attach castors to the bottom one, to create a filing system that can be wheeled in and out from under the table.

cleaning a computer

Unplug it first. Vacuum the keyboard to remove any crumbs or dust. Put some methylated spirits or lighter fuel on a cloth to clean the keys. Use a cotton bud (swab) to get in between the keys.

'No one ever said on their death bed "I wish I'd spent more time at the office".'

Rob Parsons

Right: *If working from home is a full-time, permanent arrangement, try to choose a room on which the door can be closed, to ensure work is undisturbed by the rest of the family.*

Below: *A home office can be as simple as a sunny corner of the house containing a garden table and chair, a noticeboard and a spare surface on which to put paperwork.*

Studying at home

Many households these days are acquiring computers, to the extent that they are becoming indispensable to adults and children alike. Some families even have to impose rota systems, to ensure that each person has a turn. However, the technological revolution has occurred so rapidly that many parents are worried about their children's use of computers.

There is no doubt that information available on the Internet can be valuable for schoolwork, but children have to be taught how to browse the World Wide Web efficiently, otherwise they can spend hours glued to the screen with nothing to show for it. In addition, they must be taught not to disclose information such as telephone numbers, addresses or passwords. Many parents' biggest concern is to ensure that children do not have access to inappropriate material. Software packages are available that monitor usage or restrict access to designated types of Web site, but these blocking programs, though useful, are no substitute for close parental supervision.

Sitting at a computer can be a solitary and passive activity, but if you join your child at the keyboard you can at least make it communal. Computer games often involve communal activity, too, but it's obviously important to supervise closely what games a child has access to, since a vast number are of dubious value or possibly even harmful. Finally, even if children are using the computer 'for homework' or are using an 'educational' or word-processing program, you will probably want to limit the time they spend not just online but using the computer at all. Like television, it is stopping them from doing something more active both physically and mentally.

Homework may not seem so important when children are young, and it's tempting to allow youngsters to let it slide. However, bad habits are more difficult to shift as children get older, so it's important that they learn at an early age the self-discipline required to concentrate and get their work done on time. Parents have a crucial role to play in encouraging their children. Forcing them is not the answer – children learn better if they are enjoying themselves and if the motivation is coming from within.

At the beginning, they will need a lot of help in structuring their after-school timetable, to fit in homework at the most productive time and still leave time

Far left: *If working at home is a permanent, full-time occupation, an entire room will probably need to be turned into an office. If the computer is used for business, children should not be allowed to play games on it without permission.*

Left : *Many children now do homework on a computer, which is good for developing computer skills, but you should make sure they don't abandon handwriting and researching in books.*

for other activities. Children work in different ways, so you'll have to discover by trial and error what suits them best. You could perhaps divide the homework time into a half-hour session and a 15-minute session with a break in between. Even if time is short, don't urge children to start homework as soon as they return from school – they will need a break and perhaps a snack first. For children who find it hard to get started, beginning with an easy piece of homework is a good idea, rather than having to tackle the most daunting item first. Nevertheless, they should be encouraged not to leave the hardest piece of homework to the end, when they will have run out of time, energy and patience.

While children are still developing their homework skills, you will have to find out how much they have each day, so that you can help them to plan their time. Get them to teach you about what they have learned. Not only does this allow you to become involved and find out what they should be doing, but it also reinforces and deepens their own knowledge of the subject. The challenge is to be available to help without interfering, so that children gradually become self-motivated and independent and learn to do their homework with little prompting or help from you.

Right: *Encourage younger children to learn by making it into a game, and give Teddy a desk too!*

Below left: *The kitchen table can be an ideal place for young children to do homework. There is plenty of space, and the presence of other people around them may actually help them concentrate.*

Below right: *Encourage good study habits by giving a child their own desk. Make it a 'grown-up' desk with a lamp, pinboard and pencil holder. It's important for children to have a space where it is easy for them to concentrate, without toys all around or the television blaring. You could allow them some music in the background instead.*

Bedtime

Children love familiarity and routine – it provides an anchor in their lives, makes the world seem safe and predictable, and builds up their confidence. Going to bed in their own bedroom surrounded by their favourite things creates a strong sense of security, and a regular bedtime routine forms a major part of that experience. Its importance is reflected in the fact that it usually becomes an abiding childhood memory. The habit of, say, having a bath, cuddling with Mum or Dad, saying prayers or hearing a favourite story is also an effective way of winding down after the excitement of the day and getting into a sleepy state of mind.

With all children, no matter how set the bedtime routine, there will be times when they just don't want to cooperate. Staying up late like teenagers and adults has an irresistible appeal, and if older brothers or sisters are still up, or a favourite television programme is on, it becomes even more difficult to persuade the young ones to go to bed. Getting overexcited at bedtime, running around, playing boisterous games and having pillow fights, is another cause of bedtime difficulties. The only solution in all of these situations is for parents to be utterly inflexible, so that the bedtime routine becomes set in stone and children know there is no point in attempting to alter it. Insist on a time to be in bed by, and another a little later for lights out. A rigid bedtime will keep a child's internal clock in order, and make life much easier for everyone.

If children have friends to sleep over at weekends or during school holidays, you will obviously have to make an exception to the rule. They will adore sharing the intimate moments of bedtime with their friends, talking when the lights are out and exchanging stories and secrets. But don't count on their getting much sleep.

Left: When friends come to stay, bedtime routines fly out the window. Resign yourself to the fact that they will be so excited that they won't get much sleep (nor will you), and make the best of it. After all, there's nothing like a good pillow fight – it's a good way to burn off excess energy before bedtime. Just keep an eye on things from a distance to make sure proceedings don't get out of hand.

Children's rooms

A child's bedroom should be their own personal space, somewhere they can develop, discover and express their own interests and personality. This is far more important than for the room to have an attractive colour scheme, look stylish or fit into the style of the rest of the house (all factors that a design-conscious parent may be unable to resist thinking about!).

The familiarity of a childhood bedroom is very reassuring and helps build a sense of identity as well as a feeling of security. It provides a safe base for venturing out into the world. A favourite pillowcase, teddy bear or toy box, or even a picture hanging on the wall, can in years to come evoke strong sentimental memories of a happy childhood. A young child's bedroom will probably also become part of their imaginary world. A place with secret hiding places and dens, it is the room where toys come alive. The bed may be a treasure ship one day, a spacecraft or a bus another. One corner of the room might be a shop selling sweets with pretend money, or perhaps a hospital to mend sick teddies. The space in the middle of the room will an ideal arena for horse jumping or playing with train sets, soldiers, games or plastic building blocks.

As a child grows older, their bedroom becomes even more important. It is particularly important for a teenager to have their own individual space, where they can be alone, entertain friends, listen to music and develop their own style and individuality (see page 54).

It is the walls in particular that express a child's hobbies and passions of the moment. As the child grows up, images of animals or cartoon characters will be replaced by sporting heroes, pop stars or movie pin-ups. Their room is also a place to display their achievements in the form of certificates, medals, and trophies, as well as photographs, postcards and mementoes of special times and places.

Children's bedrooms are often the messiest rooms in the house – not surprisingly, as it's difficult for a room to be tidy all the time if they want to play in it. Nevertheless, it's not unreasonable to expect them to hang up their clothes and make up the bed every day and to tidy it regularly. Children need to be taught how to look after their possessions – permanent chaos does not have to be their natural state. Provide useful storage (see page 53) and design the room so that tidying things away is quick and easy. Sometimes it even happens that games you don't particularly like are so well cleared away that they are forgotten about completely.

Left: *Stable doors on their bedrooms create a wonderful combination of privacy and togetherness for these three sisters. While the girls can chat to each other, they can still close the bottom sections to define their private space.*

Right: *Encourage children to be involved in decorating their rooms, perhaps choosing colours or fabrics. The pegs for this simple window blind could be used for hanging scarves and jewellery during the teenage years.*

Below: *An effective way to create a light but colourful bedroom is to paint the ceiling and top two thirds of the wall white and the bottom part of the wall in a colour. The lower section also hides sticky finger marks.*

Teddy bears

Teddy bears and other soft toys can play an important part in a child's life. Whether a child has dozens or just a few, there are bound to be particular favourites. The 'top' toy will be given prime position on the bed and probably have to sleep in the bed at night too. Sad is the day when Teddy is relegated from the bed to the top shelf because the child feels too 'grown up'. Until then, these toys offer a strong sense of comfort and reassurance. However threadbare, worn or scruffy, a favourite bear is a best friend for life – even after it is on the shelf. A young child will talk to the teddy, include it in games, confide in it and take it everywhere. Woe betide any parent who leaves it behind in a shop.

Above left: *A favoured teddy has been carefully tucked up in its own bed – a cot right next to the child's own bed. This is a particularly good idea if a very fragile old teddy belonging to a parent has been handed down to the child.*

Left: *A collection of Indian puppets from her parents' travels makes a striking wall decoration in this girl's bedroom. Adults often forget how much a gift from parents or mementoes from holidays can mean to children, for whom every experience is fresh and strong.*

Just as children should be responsible for their own possessions, they should be in control of their own toys and should look after them. Most youngsters like to hoard things. A child will find a secret place to store a favourite box, sticker collection or doll. Special souvenirs, like a postcard from a holiday, birthday card from Mum and Dad or matchbox containing a shiny copper coin will all reappear years later. Allow children to have their own secret places in their rooms where nobody in the family will pry.

Encourage children to give their teddies names. It doesn't need to be a contest for the most imaginative, but thinking of unusual names can be fun. They could name each teddy after the person who gave it to them, or if it is from two people, the name could be a hybrid of both their names. It could even be named after the place it was purchased or a particular event.

Right: *Well-loved soft toys are often given prime position at the head of the bed. Usually the least glamorous, most threadbare teddies are the most loved.*

Decorating children's rooms

Encourage a child to assist you with the decoration of their bedroom, to be involved in creating their own personal space. If they are old enough they can help choose colours and fabrics. If they have brothers or sisters, it will be important for them to create a room very different from their siblings' rooms.

Children's bedrooms do receive a lot of wear and tear, so don't choose anything too smart and expensive. Also avoid choosing anything aimed at a particular age, unless you relish having to redecorate in a couple of years when the child's tastes have outgrown your choice. Also, wallpaper can be difficult because Blu-Tack used to mount posters on the wall can make the wallpaper peel off, and children might lie in bed helping the process along.

It's far better, and easier, to create a colourful blank canvas on which they can express their own personality. Simply paint the walls a bright colour and add a special duvet cover and pillowcase. A painted wall is also quicker to clean or change to a different colour.

Top left: *No matter how exotic the decor, there's always a place for special soft toys.*

Left: *Simple finishing touches like colourful Indian fabric give this room its distinctive character, which would appeal to girls of all ages. The exotic bed treatment is echoed by the fabric attached to the ceiling. A large, colourful flag could be an effective alternative for a boy's room.*

Right: *The fabric is simply tucked under the mattress to make the decorative valance. With such a strong fabric, it's important to choose a colour scheme that complements it.*

Furnishing children's rooms

Because children are permanently on the go, swinging, climbing, bouncing, performing and playing, a child's room will undergo constant wear and tear. It is therefore a good idea for the furniture in a child's bedroom to be robust and inexpensive.

There is a truly exciting range of children's beds in all shapes and styles to choose from today. For a small room, there are bunk beds and high platform beds with storage or a desk and den space underneath and fun ladders to climb, as well as more sedate beds with a truckle bed hidden underneath, ready to pull out when a friend comes to stay. A child can even sleep in a bed disguised as a boat or a spaceship. However, more conventional beds can be just as nice if given an appealing duvet or bedcover. Whichever type you choose, be sure it has a good, supportive mattress. Babies and toddlers get very fond of their cots, so don't be in too much of a hurry to move a youngster into a full-sized bed. Usually, two years is about the right age. Initially, they will need a guard rail to stop them from rolling out of bed at night (and stop them from worrying about it).

Storage can be simple and basic, such as baskets, plastic boxes and lots of shelves. You may prefer to hide most of the shelves behind smart curtains or blinds or inside fitted cupboards, but a child will certainly want some open shelves for displaying treasured possessions. Baskets or drawers that fit under the bed and boxes that stack on top of each other are all practical and easy to tidy away. There needs to be storage not only for toys but for books and clothes as well. To avoid having to replace the wardrobe at a later date, choose one with enough hanging space for adult-length clothes, even though a young child's clothing will require much less room. As a child grows up, storage requirements will change, with boxes of building bricks making way for a desk perhaps, and a doll's house superseded by a dressing table.

A child needs an area of wall in their bedroom where they can display their own artwork, posters, photographs or mementos. The best arrangement is to make a giant pinboard by covering a large wall space with cork so their pictures can be put up without ruining the paintwork or wallpaper.

If there is space, make a reading corner by joining two child-height bookshelves at right angles; attach them to the walls so they cannot be pulled over. Place child-sized chairs or squashy floor cushions next to them. Adding a small table will turn it into an activity corner. Keep the main part of the room free to create an arena for playing.

Furnishing teenagers' rooms

A teenager's room needs to function as a combined bedroom, study and den. Where space is small, this can be a challenge, particularly as teenagers seem to have much more in the way of clothes, shoes, sports equipment, books, school work, sound systems, CDs, souvenirs and general junk than younger siblings.

Apart from efficient storage, which is absolutely essential, the key is to adapt furniture for more than one purpose. Make up the bed so that it looks like a daybed and can be used like a sofa, and add seating such as a futon that can be folded up for sitting on or spread out for sleeping. Supplement this seating with big cushions and beanbags that can be heaped up in the corner or on the bed when not in use.

Other important considerations are to make sure that the work surface is adequate for the teenager's study requirements and that there is good lighting for studying and for reading. Additional power points will probably be needed if there is a sound system, computer and television in the room.

Below left: *A teenager may not go so far as to hang a 'Keep Out' notice on the door, but their room is a very personal, private space, and it's important to respect this.*

Below: *No matter how small the room is, it's essential to include space for displaying photos, trophies and medals or other prized possessions. The table pictured here is like a shrine to favourite sports.*

Right: *A daybed by the window provides a good place for reading or lounging – though clothes strewn carelessly around the teenager's room are inevitable in every household.*

Bedtime stories

There is no substitute for parents and children sharing good books. It is a much more intimate and interactive experience than watching television, a film or a video. Not only are they sharing an interesting story, but there is also comforting physical contact as the child snuggles on a parent's lap or nestles in their arms to read the story. They will look forward to and treasure these special moments.

A regular routine of bedtime stories is a wonderful way to inspire in children a love of books. The comfort of a parent's warm arms and their familiar voice creates for the children a safe and happy environment, and they will always associate this sense of pleasure with reading.

Reading for pleasure makes learning fun, too. Stories open up an entire new world, so that reading becomes an adventure in itself. Encourage interaction between children and books. Read aloud to each other. Get them to look closely at the pictures and ask them questions about the books. Imitate funny voices for the characters when reading – and never get tired of reading a story to them even if it is for the hundredth time!

Right: *Storytime can become a familiar daily routine before bedtime, an intimate time between parent and child. Children will look back with great fondness on those times spent listening to a story wrapped in a parent's arms.*

Above and far right: *A story does not just have to come from a book. Children love make-believe and will enjoy a totally made-up story, especially if they are part of it or help to tell it. Make up a story that includes the child and their favourite toys or teddies. It could become an ongoing saga, where each week there is a new adventure based on the same theme and characters.*

Sharing rooms

Sharing a room may be necessary when space is at a premium in a home, and sometimes children prefer it even when they could each have their own rooms. They usually enjoy the companionship, and it can be comforting when a sibling is nearby at night – particularly for a child who has previously suffered from nightmares or feared the dark. Sharing works best when the children are close in age, but whatever their age, they will probably want their own separate zones for sleeping and doing homework, with a communal area for play. To divide the room into separate sections, you could use a storage unit with access from both sides, floor-to-ceiling shelving, a concertina divider that opens and shuts, or even a venetian blind.

Bunk beds are the easiest way to fit two beds into a small space, and children usually love them. Climbing the ladder is like getting into a tree house or a boat, while the bottom bunk is like a secret den. It is not advisable to let a young child sleep on the top bunk, as they cannot easily get down on their own. Therefore, the older child will have to sleep on the top bunk initially, and it must have a bar or barrier to stop the child from rolling out in the night. With some bunk beds it is possible to remove the bottom bunk at a later date and replace it with a desk. Painting the child's initials on each bunk helps to reinforce the idea that each child has their own territory in a shared room.

Below left: Bunk beds are ideal for children's rooms as they make it easy to fit two beds into one room. Children love climbing up to play on the top one, where they feel safely out of the reach of adults.

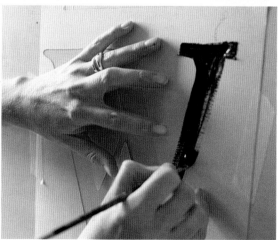

stencilled letters

Any items of furniture can be stencilled, including bunk beds, toy chests and cupboard doors. Letters are easy to do, and children love seeing their name or initial – it make them feel special.

➤ *Type the required letter as big as possible on a word processor and print it out. If it is not large enough, enlarge it on a photocopier. Carefully cut the letter out and stick it, with glue, on a piece of card to make the stencil. Choose card that is not so flimsy that it will tear but not so stiff that it cannot easily be cut with a craft knife.*

➤ *Place a cutting mat or thick cardboard underneath the card. Using a metal ruler if possible along the straight lines, carefully cut with a craft knife around the outside of the letter to leave in the card a hole shaped like the letter.*

➤ *Place the stencil in the correct position on the surface and tape it in place with masking tape.*

➤ *Neatly paint in the shape through the stencil, using a dabbing action and even strokes so that the paint does not go under the edge. Carefully remove the stencil without smudging. Leave to dry and apply a layer of varnish if you have used acrylic or emulsion (latex) paint.*

Midnight feasts and sleepovers

The first time a child has a friend to stay the night is an exciting occasion. The child realizes that the friend, who may be feeling nervous and a little homesick, is placing a special trust in them. Equally, the friend is honoured to be sharing the child's bedroom and favourite toys and secrets. It is an expression of their friendship to be able to reach a level of trust where they can share these things with each other.

As children get older, sleepovers become popular, particularly for birthday parties. Several children will come and stay at once and will all want to sleep in the same room, no matter how tightly they will be crammed in. It may therefore be necessary to turn the living room or family room into a dormitory. You could ask the children to bring their own roll-up mattresses and sleeping bags, but if you wish to provide some soft surfaces, a camp bed, an inflatable mattress, a futon, sofa cushions, or a mattress normally kept under the bed or rolled up and stored in a cupboard, would be suitable. After an evening of snacks and videos, the youngsters will love talking in the dark late into the night, making patterns with flashlights on the wall and having a midnight feast – don't bank on their getting too much sleep!

Half the fun of a midnight feast is the anticipation of it and the creeping through the house with a flashlight to find it. Stealing downstairs in the dead of night to raid the dark kitchen for goodies is like a secret mission, and taking them upstairs to eat in bed is also thrilling because it is normally forbidden. In reality, a parent will probably have to help a younger child with the practicalities of preparing the feast and making the fantasy come to fruition. However, if you get the food ready a few hours in advance, you can 'hide' it in a special drawer so that coming downstairs in the night to find the food still feels naughty. (This also allows you to exert some control, without the children realizing, over what food is taken to bed. But older children, unfortunately, will see through this stratagem!)

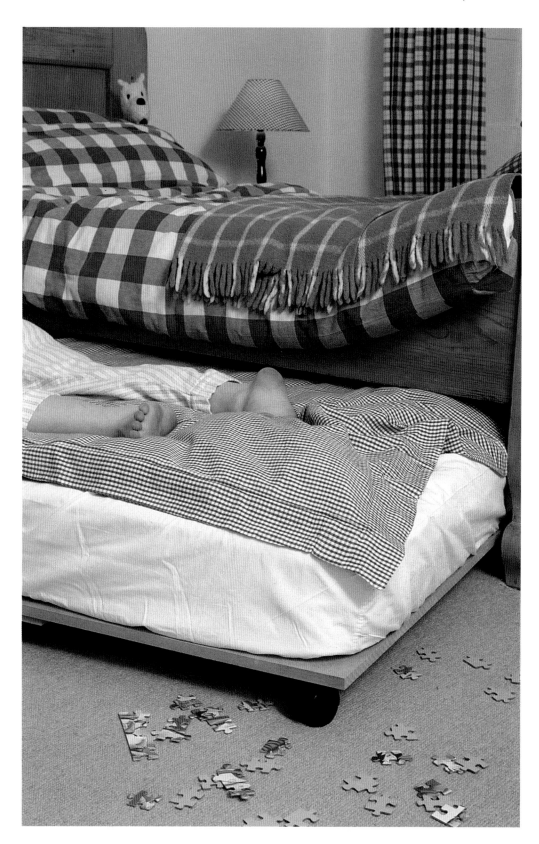

Right: *A simple way to make an instant spare bed is to cut a piece of MDF (medium-density fibreboard) to the dimensions of a mattress and attach six castors – one at each corner and one in the middle of each side. Also add a small piece of wood as a handle to pull the bed out with. Lay the mattress on top, and store under the main bed.*

Far left: *A midnight feast doesn't have to be literally at midnight. In fact, it might be a good alternative to supper, provided an adult prepares the feast so it doesn't consist entirely of junk food.*

Left: *Find some special boxes for the midnight feast, and wrap the goodies in small parcels to be opened up – having to unwrap them makes it all the more exciting for the children.*

Parents' bedrooms

The bedroom is probably the one and only room in a family home that you can call your own – a private domain where adult belongings and furnishings predominate. It's not just a place in which to sleep but an all-hours refuge from the hurly-burly of everyday family life, where you can relax and rejuvenate yourself in comfort and relative peace.

Of course, children won't be banned completely from the room, but you can make it clear to them that it is your personal space. Don't let them keep toys or games there permanently, or play in the room when you aren't there. Not only will this prevent your bedroom from becoming little more than an annex to their own rooms, but it will allow you to furnish it in a style that is not practical for children, with delicate fabrics, favourite ornaments and pale colours. In fact, it is the room of the house where you can really indulge yourself in the decoration. Whether you prefer the romantic look with a lavish use of fabric, or a contemporary minimal style with stylish neutral tones, there is enormous scope. This is the perfect outlet for all those ideas that simply wouldn't be practical anywhere else in the home. Include a comfortable chair, a small stereo and bookshelves to create a haven in which to retreat at any time of the day, even if it is just for a few minutes.

Versatile lighting is essential in a bedroom, so either combine task lighting (bedside lights for reading, bright lighting for dressing and applying make-up) with soft background lighting, or fit a dimmer switch to enable you to adjust the brightness as necessary. Candles will add a romantic atmosphere. Introduce subtle scent into the room with a pot of flowering hyacinth bulbs, a wicker basket of dried lavender or a

Below left: Most parents are familiar with the sound of pattering feet coming towards their bedroom early in the morning. Make it a special weekend treat for the children to dive into bed with their parents. It is moments like this that everyone will look back on and treasure in the future – children outgrow it far too quickly.

Below: Treat yourself to extra accessories for the bed to make it really cosy. This throw was made from a plain cream blanket. A wide border of velvet was sewn around the edge and the initials were embroidered in chunky wool.

Right: Make the bedroom a place free from the clutter of daily family life – a romantic haven of peace.

scented geranium, and you could plant up a window box with night-scented stocks outside in the summertime.

To create as much usable space in the bedroom as possible, plan storage carefully and make the most of any less obvious storage opportunities. For example, the bedside table pictured on the left is a simple wooden shelving unit dressed up with a hand-made fabric cover to hide its useful shelves. If a framed mirror was hung on the wall above the bedside table it could also double as a dressing table. But whatever else you include in the room, the bed will be the focus. Make it even more inviting by piling up extra cushions or pillows and layering on soft, warm throws – these not only look good but add a great deal to the comfort on those rare occasions when there's time to read in bed.

Of course, bedrooms are used not just at night but also in the daytime for a variety of purposes – therefore, the more amenities you can fit in, the better. If the room is spacious enough, you could perhaps incorporate a dressing room, or at least a separate dressing area. Bookshelves could be more than a mere receptacle for bedtime reading – you could extend them from floor to ceiling, perhaps in an alcove or a corner, and then place a comfortable armchair in front, to create a cosy library atmosphere and a perfect spot for a quiet read. Even without the bookcase, you could make a snug sitting area with just one or two armchairs and a lamp.

Alternatively, you might want to devote a corner of the room to fitness apparatus such as an exercise bike or a treadmill. Some people include a desk in the bedroom, in order to use the room as an office – but this will then negate the room's primary function as a retreat away from everyday chores. If at all possible, it's better to keep any important paperwork away from the bedroom and make it purely a relaxing place to switch off completely from the pressures of responsibility.

Left: *This pretty table consists of inexpensive self-assembly shelves covered with thick white cotton fabric, with the front flap edged in velvet ribbon piping. Strips of ribbon have been attached to tie the flaps closed.*

'My people will live in peaceful dwelling places, in secure homes, in undisturbed places of rest.'

Isaiah

'God bless the inventor of sleep, the cloak that covers all men's thoughts, the food that cures all hunger, the water that quenches thirst, the fire that warms cold.'

Miguel de Cervantes

eucalyptus heart wreath

This simple wreath is an effective wall decoration and would also make a nice hand-made gift, particularly as children can help to make it. Eucalyptus twigs are ideal because it dries very well. Use fresh branches, as dry ones are not flexible; the eucalyptus will dry naturally on the wall.

❥ *Bend two narrow bundles of eucalyptus branches to form the two sides of a heart, with the pairs of ends overlapping. Ask children to hold them in this position for you.*

❥ *Tie the ends together with wire or raffia where they cross at the top and bottom.*

❥ *You will need to use invisible wire, such as fishing line, to hold the eucalyptus in a heart shape and prevent the sides from straightening out. Attach one length of wire to run vertically between the two points, and a second to run horizontally between the two sides.*

Bathtime

Family life revolves around the daily routines of living, and 'bathtime' is one of those familiar words that many children can relate to. It can be an exciting time of day for them. Children love being naked: they feel liberated. No longer constricted by clothes, they are stripped of responsibility and love just running around. For some children, though, bathtime is not so welcome, because it signifies the end of playtime and time to go to bed, whereas they want to continue playing or to stay up as late as the grown-ups. It is up to parents to overcome this unpleasant association and make bathtime something to look forward to.

For the first years of childhood, bathtime can be quite a social activity. Young children have to be supervised, so a parent is involved, and some siblings have a bath at the same time. For the first years of childhood, bathtime can be quite a social activity. Young children have to be supervised, so a parent is involved, and some siblings have a bath at the same time. Older babies can join in the fun, too, provided an adult is continuously present. (Even if a young child is bathing with a baby brother or sister, they should not be left unsupervised for a moment.) The games played in the bath, the chats with a parent and the cuddles on a knee in a warm towel are all part of the well-loved routine. As children get older, however, they begin to want some privacy.

Left: *A child quickly grows too old to share a bath with siblings, so while they are young, make the most of enjoying bathtime together as a family, playing games, singing songs, splashing water. Make it a time of day to look forward to.*

Below: *Give each member of the family a different-coloured facecloth to wash with. Give them a toothbrush to match so there is never any confusion over which one to use.*

Considering how basic are the fittings that bathrooms contain, it's surprising how much they can vary, and how different families' bathing habits can be. Some families prefer showers and a highly functional space well protected against lots of water splashes. Others have opted for sybaritic rooms designed for comfort and relaxation, with a deep bath, a carpet and a comfortable chair.

If the bathroom is used more by the children than by adults, decorate it in a style that is appealing to them. Paint it in bright colours, decorate the walls with fun pictures of fish or boats and fill a basket with a choice of plastic bathtime toys. Children will not be able to resist splashing water around, however closely they are supervised, so the walls will have to be protected. Tiles are the most waterproof surface for a bathroom, but painted and varnished MDF (medium-density fibreboard) panels or tongue-and-groove panelling around the bath work well too. For the walls, bathroom paints are now available which are more resistant to mould growth resulting from humidity and superfluous water than ordinary paints.

Bathroom surfaces are very slippery so falling is a major hazard here, particularly with young children. If there is a rug or bathmat on the floor, put a non-slip underlay beneath it. You'll also need a non-slip mat in the bottom of the bath. Other safety measures are, of course, to keep electrical flexes and sockets out of the bathroom and put medicines and razors well out of children's reach, preferably high up in a locked cupboard. Younger children should be supervised at all times when in the bath, so it might be an idea to put a chair in the bathroom so a parent can supervise and assist with a

bathtime canvas

Bare plaster walls make an ideal bath drawing board. Frame an area of bare plaster with wood and paint around it. The children can draw on the plaster with wet fingers and make shapes with wet sponges. The water is quickly absorbed to leave the 'canvas' blank again.

Right: *Bathtime for younger children should be supervised by an adult. Make it a special treat to have a bath in 'Mummy's bath'. It can be a good time of day for parent and child to sit and chat together.*

degree of comfort. Young children need help washing, and shampooing hair has to be a careful operation to ensure that the stinging detergent does not get in the eyes.

Some children take to the bath like ducks to water – they will easily jump in and out, splash around, giggle and blow bubbles. But for those who need enticing into the bath, there are a wealth of bath toys, waterproof books, clockwork animals, scuba-diving dolls and squidgy sponges in bright colours and exotic animal shapes. Many children love lots of bubbles. Foamy bubbles make great beards, hats and snowmen! Make your own bath toy by filling an old squeeze bottle with water and squirting water around, or find a pot of bubbles to blow into the bath.

Once children are in the bath, it may be difficult to get them out again. Try closing your eyes and counting to three. The last resort is, of course, to pull the plug out, which usually has an instantaneous effect. Once they are out,

continue the fun. Put them on your knee, wrapped in a towel and jump them up and down singing a song. Play peekaboo with the towel as you dry their hair. If you put the pyjamas on the radiator or heated towel rail first, they will be toasty and warm when the child is ready to put them on. Finally, wrap the child in a dressing gown ready for bed.

Teach children from as early an age as possible how important it is to keep their teeth clean. Young children will need guidance to make sure they do it properly; seek advice from your dentist or hygienist on this, and ask them to show the child the proper procedure. Using an egg-timer can be a fun way to help to ensure they brush their teeth for a long enough time (two minutes is the time dentists recommend for each toothbrushing session). Blow-drying or brushing hair may also be necessary, providing a good opportunity for a child to learn how to be patient and sit still.

Left and below right:
Teeth should be
cleaned at least twice
a day, without fail –
and if possible also
after meals and after
eating sweet things.
Young children
shouldn't use adult
toothpaste as they
tend to swallow it, so
buy children's flavoured
toothpaste. A fun
toothbrush will also
help to make cleaning
teeth more appealing.

Far right: Sew strips of
fabric onto the edges
of towels so everyone
knows whose towel
is whose. These
decorative borders are
a fun way to spice up
plain towels.

Left: *Deep, hot water and scented bubbles will help the body unwind while soft, flickering candlelight will relax the mind.*

Right: *Even if your bathroom is strictly functional, a few scented candles, some pretty glass bottles of colourful bath oils, and soothing music in the background will miraculously transform the atmosphere from clinical to relaxing and peaceful.*

'A hot bath! I cry, as I sit down in it; and again, as I lie flat, a hot bath! How exquisite a vespertine pleasure, how luxurious, fervid and flagrant a consolation for the rigours, the austerities, the renunciations of the day.'

Rose Macaulay

Time to soak

A quick bath or shower – although very often a necessity – is a missed opportunity. Taking time to soak in a bath is an excellent chance for an adult to relax. It is a time for calm serenity and a rare opportunity to take time out for oneself. This is when you can wash the cares and responsibilities of the day away, down the plughole.

Methodically following your own personal bathtime ritual is a good way to make yourself feel pampered. Some people prefer showers – a blast of warm water to invigorate themselves in the morning, after sport or before going out to a party. Others prefer long, luxurious baths, whether deep or shallow, with bubbles or with emollient oils. For many couples, this is a good time to chat to a partner about the day. Others favour total solitude and privacy, perhaps immediately after the children have gone to bed. Whatever your own preference, this can be an ideal time to regain your sanity and equilibrium after the trials and tribulations of the day.

It doesn't really take very much to create the ideal atmosphere for total relaxation in a bathroom. A wide range of luxurious bath additives and body lotions are available to help with this, so treat yourself to some fragrant essential oils (a small bottle can last a surprisingly long time) or bubbles. If necessary, drop heavy hints around the time of your birthday or at Christmas-time. A candlelit bath will help the mind switch from the day's problems to a more contemplative state. (Never leave the candles lit unattended or within reach of a child, though.) Play your favourite music, lie back in the warmth and relax. A glass of wine and a book are optional extras. Put clean, soft towels on the radiator or heated towel rail so they are warm when you get out – after a relaxing soak, nothing is worse than finding that the only towels to hand are damp ones used at children's bathtime!

You can create an atmosphere of comfort and warmth in a bathroom through your choice of decoration. Paint the walls in your favourite colour. Bring a comfortable, cushioned chair into the room to make a pleasant place to sit and dry yourself, or from which to chat to a spouse in the bath. Arrange some favourite objects on a shelf, such as shells and pebbles from the beach or a collection of glass, and fill a beautiful bowl with colourful, perfumed soaps. Line strong wicker baskets with fabric and display them on a shelf with all the bottles hidden neatly inside.

One essential for a serene and sensuous bathroom is efficient storage, so you can hide those essential but none too beautiful bottles of shampoo and

tubes of toothpaste. Unfortunately, bathrooms are often so small that there is little room for storage units, and considerable ingenuity may be required to fit everything in. Baskets and open shelving look attractive, or unused areas can be utilized, with, for example, a vanity unit under the basin or a cupboard behind a bath panel. In a larger bathroom there may be room for purpose-built units or freestanding furniture such as an armoire or a chest of drawers.

If space permits, the bathroom is also an ideal place for a laundry cupboard or basket. Give each member of the family their own laundry bag and hang the bags on a row of hooks. Or you could have two large laundry baskets, one for white clothes and one for coloured, so that everyone pre-sorts their own laundry. Another benefit is that it gets children into the habit of putting their dirty clothes straight into the baskets rather than scattering them around the floor.

Far left: *A large bathroom cupboard is invaluable for hiding the everyday clutter.*

Below left: *Give each member of the family their own laundry bag so they take responsibility for tidying away their own dirty laundry.*

Above: *Install two wicker laundry baskets in the bathroom and label one for white laundry and one for coloured. Even young children can learn to put their dirty clothes into the correct basket.*

Right: *Lining a basket with fabric makes for more practical and attractive bathroom storage because soft objects like cotton wool or soaps get scratched on the wicker.*

Friends to stay

Having friends or family to stay the night or for the weekend creates an opportunity to build on friendships or establish new bonds with people. The secret of good hospitality is to be relaxed and informal, and to make guests feel genuinely welcome. If you have a spare room, it shouldn't take much to turn it into a welcoming guest room. Apart from an attractively made-up bed, fluffy towels and a wardrobe with empty hangers rather than your off-season wardrobe, all it will need is a posy of fresh flowers and a jug of drinking water with glasses. A selection of newspapers, magazines and books and a bedside table with a lamp and clock are nice extra touches. Provide an extra blanket or hot water bottle to guard against chills.

A spare room isn't essential, however. A sofa-bed in the living room, family room or home office is an ideal alternative, or an ordinary sofa can be adapted with a couple of fluffy pillows, a warm duvet and some bed linen. Other ways of making an extra bed include deep self-inflating mattresses; modular furniture that can be pulled together to form a bed; extra mattresses stored under other beds; and futons.

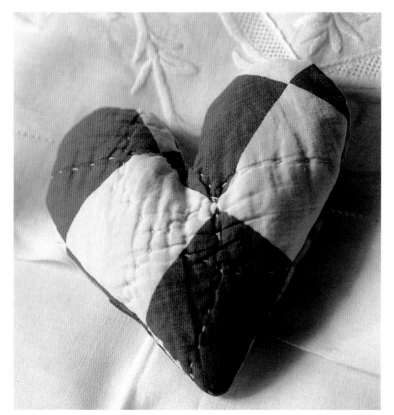

Right: *A minimally decorated room in the attic has been turned into a comfortable guest room with the simple addition of an attractively dressed bed, a bedside table with reading lamp, and some flowers.*

Far left: *The stylish headboard in the spare room featured on these pages was made from an inexpensive piece of MDF (medium-density fibreboard) covered in padding and then a tie-on ticking fabric cover that can be removed for washing. The edges of the MDF were covered with self-adhesive felt.*

Left: *Small personal touches like a lavender bag on the pillow or flowers by the bed will make a guest room more welcoming.*

Outdoor living

In the summertime, when the weather is balmy, the arena in which family life takes place stretches beyond the walls of a house or apartment into the great outdoors. Gardens, balconies and roof gardens all extend the living space of a home, providing a wonderful place to relax, play, entertain, dine and work. On a sunny day, you can spread out your work on a table and create an instant office, or scatter rugs and cushions on the lawn and use it as an outdoor living room. At the weekend, children can pitch a tent and turn the garden into a bedroom.

Even a humblest garden shed can be turned into an outdoor retreat. Clear out all the junk that tends to accumulate and give the shed a thorough spring clean. Jazz it up with a coat of paint and add some seating. Wicker furniture that is no longer smart enough to live indoors is ideal; dress it up with some soft cushions and a cosy throw so that it can still be used when the weather turns a little chilly. Lighting can be provided either by standard overhead light or by more romantic candles in the form of lanterns. Add a table to house books, newspapers, drinks and perhaps a vase of home-grown flowers.

Enjoying the outdoors is one of the easiest things a family can do together. As we all spend so much time indoors, it is vital for people to make time to enjoy activities in the fresh air. Even a small garden produces a sense of freedom – children feel less confined by conventional codes of behaviour. Just being able to run, skip, hop or jump is enough for them, but, in fact, the outdoors offers a wealth of activities for any family member, from playing on swings or enjoying a lively game of cricket or baseball, to gardening or even just strolling. Physical activity is not only good for everybody, whatever their age, but it is something that can be shared with friends and family.

Above left: Transform a garden shed or other outbuilding with a coat of paint, a couple of comfortable chairs and a table, making it a delightful retreat from the house in warm weather.

Left: A pile of cushions and a few throws will make a hard wicker chair just as inviting as any armchair.

Right: Any partially enclosed outdoor room, whether it is an outbuilding, a porch, a gazebo or some other structure, allows you to enjoy the garden in comfort, protected from fierce sun and rain alike.

Family Food

Mealtimes are the anchor of daily family life – the times in the day
when everyone takes a break from a busy schedule to gather together.
Sitting around the same table, sharing food, is a wonderful symbol
of the unity of the family.

*In some families, breakfast times rarely coincide on a weekday, but for others
the meal is a chance to touch base and share plans for the day,
even if everyone is a little sleepy.*

Weekday breakfasts 86

Weekend breakfasts 89

Packed lunches 92

Picnics 95

Weekend lunches 97

Feeding a crowd 99

After-school tea 102

Kids in the kitchen 106

Friends to tea 104

Happy and healthy eating 109

Family suppers 111

There's no getting round the need for some meals to be fast and functional. Fulfilling our fundamental needs for sustenance, they are designed to fill the energy gap quickly and efficiently so that we can get on with all the tasks for the day. Because they tend to be at wildly different times, family members often wind up eating alone in whatever brief slot they can fit into their busy days.

Other meals, however, are more leisurely and sociable and, with luck, take place when everyone is at home and ready to eat. These are the times when people come together to share good food and conversation. For a family, these mealtimes can be symbolic. An evening meal in particular might be the only time all day when the entire family shares the same activity. Everyone leaves their work behind and relaxes. Sitting around a table together, family members are face to face, creating an ideal forum for enjoying conversation and banter, as well as good food. Mealtimes also tap into the basic human instinct of nurturing. Providing food is a way of showing our love for someone. It's very satisfying watching the family all together tucking into a meal with gusto.

Of course, mealtimes require a lot of work, with never-ending menu-planning, shopping, cooking, and clearing up afterwards. It can also take a lot of effort to make the meals themselves run smoothly. But although it may sometimes be a battle to get all the family involved in the preparation and clearing up, this can all be an enjoyable part of the mealtime ritual. Take ideas from these pages and feel inspired afresh by family mealtimes.

Weekday breakfasts

Breakfast can be a busy time of day for a family. Children have to be woken up, dressed, fed and got ready for school all in the space of an hour or less. Even just getting them out of bed can be a huge feat in itself, particularly if they are teenagers. Nor is early morning always the easiest time for good communication.

However, breakfast is the most important meal of the day, especially for growing children. The chances are that if you have younger children, they will need help and encouragement to eat a nourishing breakfast. And if they are not particularly good at eating their packed lunches or school dinners, then a decent breakfast is even more important. Without it, they become tired quickly and lose concentration. For many families, toast or cereal is all that anyone feels like. The children will help themselves and then bury their heads behind the cereal packets, the backs of which somehow always seem to fascinate a half-asleep person.

Nutritionally it is important for young children to have full-fat milk, not skimmed or semi-skimmed. If you can't get them to drink milk on its own, you might have to resort to flavoured milks and yogurts, which tend to be popular with children. Bear in mind, though, that once they have got used to, say, chocolate milk, it may be extremely difficult to persuade them to return to the plain variety.

Breakfast is a good opportunity to give children some fruit, either in the form of a glass of juice, or perhaps as a sliced banana on cereal, or sliced peaches, bananas, strawberries and grapes with yogurt. For children who are in a rush, a milkshake made in the blender from a banana, a glass of milk and a teaspoon of honey is a quick but healthy breakfast.

In the winter, hot oat-based cereals go down very well, as they are warming, easy to eat and delicious with a spoonful of honey, golden syrup or melted brown sugar on top. Eggy bread, or French toast, is many a child's favourite breakfast. Just soak a piece of bread in a beaten egg, then lightly fry it in butter – it's delicious topped with honey or maple syrup.

Top left: Setting the kitchen table for breakfast the night before can save valuable time in the mornings.

Bottom left: It is essential that children eat something before setting off for school, even if it is just a thick slice of toast smothered in peanut butter or jam, and washed down with a mug of fruit juice.

Right: By getting up just a few minutes earlier in the morning, everyone can gather together, however briefly, for a meal that will set them up for the day.

'When you wake up in the morning, Pooh,'
said Piglet, 'what's the first thing you say
to yourself?'
'What's for breakfast?' said Pooh.

A A Milne, Winnie-the-Pooh

Left: *Make time for a healthy and nourishing feast to start the weekend, especially if breakfast is rushed during the week.*

Below: *A traditional fried breakfast, though not something that should be indulged in frequently, is a real treat at weekends.*

Right: *Natural yogurt drizzled with golden honey makes a great start to the day.*

Far right: *At the weekend, have something for breakfast that there is not time for in the week, such as a pile of pancakes smothered in maple syrup. Big bowls of fresh soft fruit such as berries and cherries make a good accompaniment.*

Weekend breakfasts

A leisurely breakfast is sometimes a treat only indulged in when on holiday, but it can make a relaxing way to start the weekend. Prepare a tray of food, gather a pile of newspapers or a good book and take time to chat with a partner and put the week's work far behind. Let the children make their own breakfast, even if it is only a piece of toast with peanut butter – they may not want to linger over a leisurely, grown-up breakfast anyway. The family need not eat together but can simply 'graze', and individuals can find their own food when they are hungry. Alternatively, the adults may choose to cook each other something special. Perhaps it is a chance for the person who normally organizes breakfast to relax and be cooked for. Pancakes make a delicious hot breakfast, and the children will love them, too. Cook a large pile and smother them in maple syrup, or fill them with fruit and yogurt.

Choose a peaceful spot in the home, or if it is sunny take breakfast outside. Lay the table with a nice cloth and make it a romantic meal for two. For a birthday or anniversary treat, perhaps you could have a champagne breakfast with smoked salmon and scrambled eggs. Of course, if it becomes a bigger feast and is eaten a bit later, it can easily turn into brunch, which is, by definition, a thoroughly leisurely meal.

It is relatively simple to produce an outstanding breakfast. If the full fry-up of eggs and bacon is too much, have scrambled eggs on toasted brown bread instead. Poached eggs on toasted crumpets or English muffins are delicious; or try eggs Benedict, which combines the poached eggs and crumpets with ham and hollandaise sauce.

A delicious, healthy, organic feast, which there may not be time to prepare during the week, becomes a delight. Live yogurt is good for the digestive system and is easily enlivened with lashings of fresh fruit or honey drizzled on top. Make muesli more exciting by adding slices of bananas or strawberries. Drizzle the juice from a passion fruit on cereal or yogurt.

Breakfast in bed can be a great treat. It's a fun thing to do for children on their birthdays; even better, when they are old enough teach children to make it for their parents. Grandparents usually love breakfast in bed. If they come to stay, it can become a regular ritual for youngsters to sit up in bed with a grandmother or grandfather, eat breakfast with them and perhaps share a storybook. Not only do the children and grandparents enjoy it, but the parents can have a lie-in.

Left: *Breakfast in bed is a wonderful treat. For a special occasion, jazz up some scrambled eggs with a slice of smoked salmon. Teach the children to make breakfast in bed for their parents, but as you won't be able to supervise, don't allow them to do anything that requires cooking – toast and cereal and mugs of tea are perfect.*

Below: *A pile of fresh croissants and some coffee is one of the quickest and most delicious breakfasts, and often tastes even better when eaten outside in the sun.*

Packed lunches

Many children choose not to have school dinners, so a packed lunch becomes another meal to prepare every weekday. Children should be encouraged to make their own packed lunches as soon as they are old enough to. If you have trouble getting the children motivated in the morning, insist they make it the night before.

It may be an idea to prepare a big batch of sandwiches and freeze them in individual bags. A child can grab one from the freezer each morning and it will be defrosted by lunchtime. Some fillings, such as meat, poultry, salmon, tuna, cheese or peanut butter, freeze better than others. Avoid raw vegetables, jam, mayonnaise and hard-boiled eggs in particular.

Variety and surprise are important, so ring the changes with imaginative sandwich fillings inside different sorts of rolls, fruit breads, pitta pockets, ciabatta, and baguettes, as well as granary and wholemeal breads. Fresh fruit is tailor-made for packed lunches, but children enjoy having lots of little packages to open, so also include little pots of salad or raw vegetables, boxes of raisins or other dried fruits, and cartons of juice.

There are a wealth of fun lunchboxes available these days. For non-perishables, sealable plastic containers are ideal. For yogurt and sandwiches containing meat, fish or eggs, however, it's important to use either insulated

containers – such as Thermos boxes and wide-mouthed vacuum flasks, small cool boxes and insulated bags – or refreezable portable ice packs inside the lunchboxes. Not only will this keep the food fresh but it will help avoid disasters like yogurt leaking all over school books in the satchel.

Apart from the food, there are other ways to make packed lunches more exciting. Hide a mini-toy or love note in the child's lunchbox. Put a sticker on the sandwich bundle or give the child a special treat on Fridays.

a dozen sandwich fillings

1 Sliced bananas & honey
2 Salami & cream cheese
3 Ham, chutney & sliced tomato
4 Peanut butter, crispy bacon, mustard & cress
(Roald Dahl's favourite)
5 Roast pork, apple sauce & lettuce
6 Crumbled crispy bacon, peanut butter, chopped
apple & lettuce
7 Cream cheese, ham & sliced cucumber
8 Roast beef & coleslaw
9 Chicken, mayonnaise & lettuce
10 Tuna, mayonnaise & sweetcorn
11 Cottage cheese, chopped dates & diced
red pepper
12 Edam cheese, grated carrots & raisins

Top left: *Having had an early breakfast, children are usually ravenous by lunchtime so a filling yet nutritious lunch is essential.*

Far left below: *A lunch with an American theme – peanut butter and jam sandwiches, a bag of popcorn, a flavoured milkshake and a toffee apple – will undoubtedly be greeted with rapture.*

Centre left: *Give a packed lunch a colour theme such as pink, include a pink yogurt and strawberry milk, and decorate the sandwich wrapping with pink stickers.*

Left: *Last night's leftover pasta may be delicious cold for lunch the next day. Fill different containers with a variety of goodies. Try dried fruit or apple chips as a healthier alternative to potato crisps.*

Right: *Pitta pockets make great sandwiches for children – they are easy to pack with yummy fillings and easy for the child to hold. Raisins make a healthy sweet snack.*

Picnics

The beauty of a picnic lies in its simplicity – you don't need elaborate pre-cooked food for a delicious feast. Simply fill up a basket with goodies from the kitchen, grab a picnic rug and find a beautiful sunny spot. Enjoy simple finger food, then afterwards lie back on the grass or sand, gaze at the sky and daydream away.

Picnics can be one of the easiest and simplest ways to entertain, and a wonderful excuse for family friends and relations to come together. Choose a good picnic site which is easy for everyone to find and ask each guest to bring a dish. Everybody can enjoy sharing food without one person being burdened with the catering. You can invite five people or fifty!

Picnics can also be made into special occasions. Fill up a hamper with delicious quiche, salads, bread and dips, plates and cutlery, and chilled wine. Don't forget the rugs and perhaps some comfortable cushions. If you want even more comfort (and you have enough willing helpers to carry everything), bring a fold-up table and chairs.

A night-time picnic is the stuff of childhood memories. Gather together plenty of lanterns, take them to the beach and light a campfire. Cook baked potatoes in the fire, ensuring they are well wrapped in silver foil first, and afterwards let the children toast marshmallows on long sticks over the embers as you sing songs and tell each other ghost stories.

a spur-of-the-moment picnic

All you need is some bread, a chopping board, fillings such as cheese, cold meats, tomatoes and salad, some knives, a good supply of drinks and, of course, a picnic rug. Prepare the sandwiches in situ – it saves time and complicated preparation in advance, and everybody has the satisfaction of creating their own sandwiches. The joy of a picnic, especially for families, is that you don't even need plates – all the crumbs and stray fillings can be liberally spilt on the sand or grass and it doesn't matter (as long as no litter is left). If you are at the beach, wash the plates in the sea afterwards.

Far left: *A watermelon is perfect for a picnic, especially if water is nearby, as the sticky juice can be quickly washed off with a swim. Have a competition to see who can blow the pips the furthest.*

Left: *If the picnic is on the beach it may be best to prepare the sandwiches in advance to avoid sand getting in them. Using a knife and fork can be much more difficult on a sandy beach.*

Weekend lunches

Due to work and school, family members are often unable to get together for lunch during the week, which makes a relaxed, unhurried weekend lunch a very special meal. For many families, Sunday lunch is a tradition, a time to share a delicious meal and perhaps invite grandparents or friends round. Lunch can often be more leisurely than supper – a good opportunity to grab some precious moments of quality time, to linger and chat around the table.

If friends have children of a similar age, it can be enjoyable for everyone if the youngsters are allowed to entertain themselves. They may wish to eat separately or perhaps disappear to the end of the garden or into the house, giving the adults some peace and quiet. The priority on these occasions is the conversation, but that doesn't mean the food has to be uninspiring. A big roast lunch, for example, can be quite easy to prepare, particularly if there is help with peeling vegetables. Everything can be put in the oven together and cooked slowly, with only occasional servicing (and children often prefer these straightforward meals to something more elaborate).

For people with little time to spare, simple food is preferable as it allows the cook(s) to spend more time with family and friends. Many harassed hosts forget that their guests would prefer them to spend time chatting rather than disappearing into the kitchen to prepare fiddly, impressive dishes. A menu of soup, bread, cheese and salad makes a perfect wholesome lunch at any time of year; and if the weather is warm and sunny, a light salad lunch in the garden is perfect. Making salad dressing (see right) is also an easy task for children, who love contributing something to a meal for relatives or friends.

simple salad dressing

The secret of tasty salad is a delicious dressing, which children can easily make themselves. Simply mix together the following ingredients in a screw-top jar.

2 parts olive oil to 1 part balsamic vinegar
Lots of salt and pepper
1 heaped teaspoon of crunchy golden sugar

Top right: *Roast vegetables, particularly peppers, courgettes and red onions, are very quick to prepare, are delicious with any salad and can be served hot or cold.*

Centre right: *Make a separate tomato salad, dressed with oil, vinegar and fresh herbs.*

Left and below: *On a sunny day, take the table and chairs into the garden. Find a spot with some shade for those who do not like too much sun. If it is windy, put clothespegs around the tablecloth to stop it blowing off.*

Feeding a crowd

A buffet is the perfect way to feed a crowd, particularly if you are inviting more people than can be squeezed around your table. And because everyone helps themselves and sits wherever they can find space – on the arm of a sofa, the floor, the stairs or wherever – it is certain to be a relaxed occasion. Whether entertaining families with children of all ages, or young people who are friends of your own children, the informality of a buffet makes it ideal.

The main rule for feeding a crowd is to keep the food simple but have lots of it. Not only should it be quick to prepare and not too expensive, but it's important that it is quick to serve and can be eaten easily without the need for a knife. The most straightforward menu for feeding a crowd is a cold joint of meat, baked potatoes and a selection of salads. A ham can feed many people, while the salad and potatoes take little time to prepare and are very economical. Serve some pickles, sauces and a delicious salad dressing to spice up the flavours. Have a huge basket of rustic bread, perfect for satisfying big appetites. With a simple meal like this, fifteen people can be fed as easily as five. A combination of hot and cold food works well, too, although there is more last-minute preparation to contend with. If you do offer a choice of, say, two hot main dishes, bear in mind that most people will find it impossible to choose between them and so will have both!

If you have older teenagers, the chances are you will not know if they will be joining you until they turn up at the door five minutes before the meal is ready. If this is a regular occurrence, prepare food that can easily stretch to the unexpected visitor. Pasta, pies, casseroles and joints of meat easily feed extras. Equally, when feeding a crowd it is easy to cook too much, so choose food that can be heated up the next day, such as a large stew. Cold potatoes, pasta or rice can be used up in delicious salads. Because a green salad quickly goes soggy once it is dressed, serve it with the dressing separate – that way, if it's not finished, it can go back in the fridge.

Even when you are serving simple food, very little effort is needed to make the meal special. Flowers, candles and an imaginative table setting all help to make the buffet table the focal point of the party. Be sure to involve your children in laying out the table, as well as in preparing and serving the food, and don't be afraid to ask your friends – adults and children alike – to help, too. Plan in advance which tasks you can ask them to do. As well as allowing you to see more of your guests, involving them is an excellent way to relax everyone and make them feel at home.

Top right: To create a sense of occasion with minimal effort, tie napkins in sprigs of rosemary from the garden. Rosemary is ideal because it does not wilt out of water.

Centre right: As an informal alternative to candlesticks, a bucket of sand provides an excellent solid base for candles. Children may enjoy preparing the bucket of sand, perhaps taken from their sandpit.

Bottom right: Roast vegetables are easy to cook. Simply sprinkle olive oil, salt, pepper and herbs over them and roast for at least half an hour.

Left: Cheese and cold meats are delicious with salad. They can easily be wrapped up and enjoyed for a few days if not all of them are eaten at once. A huge dish of hot pasta with a tomato sauce is a nice accompaniment so that not all the food is cold.

pumpkin soup

A hollowed-out pumpkin filled with soup looks great on a buffet table, especially if the soup is made from the pumpkin flesh. This is a fun dish to serve in autumn, at Halloween, Thanksgiving or harvest time, and children will enjoy helping to hollow out the pumpkin. Use a large pumpkin, or, if you have a smaller one, decrease the rest of the ingredients accordingly. The quantities given here will serve 8–10 people.

25g (1oz) butter and 15ml (1 tbsp) olive oil for frying	2.3L (10 cups) chicken stock
2 cloves garlic, crushed	Zest and juice of 2–3 oranges
1 onion, chopped	Crushed coriander seeds
4 potatoes, sliced	Pinch of mace and nutmeg
4 carrots, sliced	1 bay leaf
Flesh from 1 large pumpkin, cut into 2.5cm (1in) chunks	Salt & pepper
	2–3 tbsp fresh coriander, chopped, and cream, to garnish

'Cooking is about not cheating yourself of pleasure.'
Nigel Slater

❥ Melt the butter and olive oil in a large pan. Add the garlic, onion, potatoes and carrots. Sauté slowly and gently for 5–10 minutes.

❥ Add the pumpkin to the pan and cook gently for a further 10 minutes until all the vegetables are soft.

❥ Add the chicken stock, orange juice and zest, spices and seasoning and heat to boiling point, then simmer for a further 20 minutes.

❥ Liquidize in batches in a blender or food processor, then reheat. Adjust seasoning, and serve from the hollow pumpkin with cream and chopped fresh coriander.

After-school tea

After a busy day at school, children are bound to come home hungry and in need of refuelling. If they will be having supper later, all they need now is a light snack – such as a glass of milk and a muffin or a piece of toast with honey. If you can get them into the habit of heading for the fruit bowl, it will stand them in good stead for their whole lives. In the summer, healthy ice lollies – free of extra sugar, colourings and preservatives – are always popular, and they are simplicity itself to prepare. Just fill lollipop moulds with yogurt or pure fruit juice and put them in the freezer.

If tea is the children's main meal of the day, however, something more substantial is required. Pasta is always a favourite. Not only does it come in a variety of fun shapes, from bow ties and shells to letters of the alphabet, but the sauces to go on it are quick to prepare and easy to vary. Pasta sauce is a good place to hide vegetables that may be unpopular on their own. The chances are that if sprigs of broccoli are smothered in tomato sauce and hidden beneath some grated cheese, they will be eaten unnoticed. Casseroles like lasagne and shepherd's pie are easy for children to eat, and are always well liked. Dishes like these can be made in advance in a big batch and then frozen, saving a lot of daily cooking time.

Young children are notoriously fussy about their food, but you can make it more enticing by sometimes arranging the components of the meal into the shape of a clown, animal, star or whatever. Even a vague resemblance is enough – there's no need to spend hours preparing works of art. Give some of the food fun names, such as toast 'soldiers' and 'bananas in pyjamas'. Naming a dish after a favourite bear or doll is another useful ploy.

Left: Children love finger food, especially corn on the cob and these 'pizzas' made from crusty bread rather than traditional dough.

Right: For 'bananas in pyjamas', insert blocks of chocolate down the middle of bananas, wrap in foil and bake until the chocolate melts.

painting egg cups

Boiled eggs and toast 'soldiers' are a traditional children's favourite. To make them even more fun, encourage the children to decorate their own egg cups. These are also good home-made Easter or Christmas presents, and other pieces of plain crockery, such as mugs, plates, bowls and plates, can be painted, too. This kind of painting needs a steady hand, however, so it is not such a good activity for very young children.

❦ You will need plain, ovenproof egg cups, a thin brush and ceramic paint (available from art shops). Make sure you select ceramic paint that is safe to come into contact with food. Before you start, put some newspaper down to protect the surface.

❦ Suggest that the children work out what they are going to draw on a piece of paper. The design needs to be simple to be effective over such a small area. Letters or initials work well, too.

❦ Carefully paint the design on the egg cup. Any mistakes should be wiped off immediately with a damp cloth.

❦ Most ceramic paints require that the object be baked in the oven afterwards to seal the paint – check the instructions on the pots of paint you are using.

❦ To ensure the designs stay on the egg cups for as long as possible, it is advisable not to wash these items in the dishwasher.

Friends to tea

Having friends come to play and stay for tea is a lovely way for young children to meet up with other children of their own age – and it's also a good excuse for special cakes and party-type food. Making a cake for someone makes them feel special – it doesn't have to be something reserved only for birthdays. Children particularly love brightly coloured cakes covered with sweets or other decorations. (Of course, before the children tuck into the sweet things, they'll need some savoury food, like a plate of pinwheel sandwiches, mini triangles of pizza, cocktail sausages or pieces of cheese and cherry tomatoes on cocktail sticks.)

Allowing children to ice the cakes adds immensely to the fun. Stirring the icing, sticking all the decorations in place and, of course, licking the bowl is at least as enjoyable as eating the result, especially if making a real mess is part of the process! The beauty of cake decorating is that it is simple yet highly creative. Cakes can be decorated with icing in all the colours of the rainbow and with all manner of tempting goodies. Allow children to choose the colours and decorations themselves. Chocolate in any shape or form is always a favourite, and small sweets can be arranged in interesting shapes or letters. Other possible decorations include strawberries, raspberries, mandarin orange segments, grapes or other fresh fruits, as well as glacé cherries or hundreds and thousands.

Left: Reward children for their help by allowing them to lick the spoon (provided it doesn't contain traces of raw egg).

Below right: To make teatime special, get some of the children's drawings laminated – they make easy-to-clean place mats.

Below far right: Friendship bracelets are a fun alternative to napkin rings.

Right: *As a special treat, make sandwiches from sliced bread, remove the crusts and use a pastry cutter to cut the sandwiches into fun shapes.*

Far right: *Cupcakes always go down well and can be easier for a child to eat than a big slice of cake.*

Below: *Make the table appealing to children so it feels like a special meal just for them and their playmates.*

Kids in the kitchen

Cooking is an enormously satisfying creative art, and an obvious and simple one to teach children. They need to be involved in food preparation at home, as it is a skill they will need all their lives. The chances are that if they can prepare a few simple meals, they will not live off a diet of fast food when they first leave home. Start with something simple, like making pastry. Not only is it one of the safest things a child can do, but it can be creative, too. Gradually involve them in all the processes of preparing food, from stirring things to creating their own puddings. With encouragement and support, they may one day be able to cook an entire meal for the whole family.

Learning to enjoy food can involve activities other than just cooking. Take the children to the market to help with the shopping or visit a 'pick your own' farm. Picking fruit is a summer pastime whole families can enjoy together. Filling a bucket with apples or picking blackberries from the hedgerows is a good way for young children to learn where food comes from. Half the fun is eating the fruit on the way home but there will probably be enough to enjoy for several days, and it always tastes better if you have picked it yourselves.

Baking, especially cakes, is a very child-friendly activity. Children can be involved in all stages, from choosing the flavours to testing to see if it is done. The finished product can be quite dramatic and is bound to be greeted with delight by friends and family. Cake is real comfort food, not just while it is

Below: *Involve children in the whole process of food preparation, including growing and harvesting it, discovering where the food actually comes from, shopping for it, and cooking and eating it.*

apple pie

Filling:

8–10 apples

50g (2oz/¼ cup) butter

50g (2oz/¼ cup) brown sugar

Spoonful ground cinnamon

Pastry:

225g (8oz/½ cup) plain flour

100g (4oz/½ cup) butter

1 egg yolk mixed with 30ml (2 tbsp) water

125ml (½ cup) milk

❧ *For the filling, peel, core and slice the apples and put them in a saucepan with the rest of the filling ingredients. Cover and gently cook until the fruit softens, then leave it to cool.*

❧ *For the pastry put the flour and butter in a bowl. Rub and knead the butter into the flour until the butter is broken down and the texture feels soft and crumbly. Very gradually add the egg yolk and water to bind the mixture together into a dough. Be careful not to add too much, but if you do, you can add extra flour.*

❧ *Knead the dough into a smooth ball. Sprinkle flour on the surface and on the rolling pin. Roll out the dough so it is slightly larger all around than the pie dish, leaving a little extra for decorating.*

❧ *Fill the pie dish with the stewed apple, mounding it up in the centre. Brush some milk around the edge of the pie dish so the pastry will stick to it. Place the pastry lid over the dish, and push the edges down gently. Cut a couple of slits in the pastry. Cut out shapes to decorate the top of the pie, brush them with milk and stick in place. Lightly brush the pastry lid with milk to glaze it.*

❧ *Bake in a medium oven for 20–30 minutes, until the filling is hot and the pastry lightly browned.*

being eaten but also in the preparation. The whole process of filling the bowl with flour, eggs and sugar and mixing it all together is soothing and satisfying.

Cake-making is a very safe activity, as it doesn't involve the use of knives, hot saucepans or boiling water. Children will still need to be supervised, however, especially when measuring out the ingredients and taking the cake in and out of the oven. If your children are quite young, you may have to do most of the preparation, but you can give them special tasks along the way like pouring the ingredients into the bowl or stirring. If two or more youngsters are involved, make sure you divide up the tasks evenly or it can lead to squabbles. (Sharing the activity with a friend or sibling helps a young child develop not just basic measuring and cooking skills but also social skills such as cooperation.) With older children you can help them follow the recipe and let them do it all themselves, but keep a close eye to avoid accidents.

There is something symbolic in baking for family or friends. It is a simple act of showing you care for them because you have gone to the effort of creating something home-made. And there are endless excuses for making a cake – because grandparents are coming to stay, because it is the weekend or simply because you want to show someone your love for them.

Right: *Children can be in charge of spooning the madeleine mixture into the mould and sprinkling the cooked cakes with sugar.*

making madeleines

These little, shell-shaped cakes, which are baked in madeleine tins consisting of small, fluted moulds, have for centuries been loved by French children, most famously by Marcel Proust. This recipe makes 12-16 cakes.

90g (3½oz/scant ½ cup) butter	100g (4oz/1 cup) plain flour
2 eggs	5ml (1tsp) baking powder
100g (4oz/1 cup) icing sugar	Zest of 1 orange
1 vanilla pod	

❥ *Melt the butter in a saucepan over very low heat, then let it cool.*

❥ *Combine the eggs with the icing sugar and vanilla pod, and beat for 5 minutes. Remove the vanilla pod. Sieve the flour and baking powder into the egg mixture. Beat for 5 minutes. Add the melted butter and orange zest and leave the mixture in the fridge for 15 minutes.*

❥ *Preheat the oven to 200°C (400°F/gas 6). Grease and flour the madeleine tin, and spoon the mixture into the individual moulds, which should be two-thirds full. Bake for 12–15 minutes.*

❥ *Remove the madeleines from the tin, cool on a wire rack and then dust with icing sugar. Eat when freshly baked if possible.*

'And suddenly the memory revealed itself. The taste was that of the little piece of madeleine which on Sunday mornings... my aunt Léonie used to give me, dipping it first in her own cup of tea...'

Marcel Proust, Swann's Way

Happy and healthy eating

However varied the food children are given, there are bound to be phases when they become picky and refuse to eat certain foods. The challenge for parents is to make sure children are encouraged to eat a healthy, balanced diet yet do not become spoiled and demanding as a result. Parents have to take a no-nonsense approach, but without making mealtimes a battleground.

Nearly all children are picky about vegetables. It is better to find out which vegetables they do like and then provide plenty of them, than to have a tantrum over some broad beans. Children's taste buds develop in time, so even if they do not like Brussels sprouts when they are four, they may love them by the time they are fourteen. If they are made to eat something they do not like, it can destroy a taste for it for life. The difficulty comes in discerning whether they really do dislike what you have given them or are just causing a scene to get your attention or assert their independence.

Compromise is often a good option. Ask them to eat three more mouthfuls rather than finish the whole plate; three mouthfuls are easily quantifiable in a child's mind. Remove the skins from fruit and vegetables, and cut them into bite-size mouthfuls so they are easy to digest and chew. Similarly, mashed potato, which is lovely and gooey and soft, is easier for young children to eat than roast or baked potatoes with crackly bits of skin. Let them dip things in ketchup if it helps the fish-finger or vegetable go down. Most important of all, try to avoid cajoling the child or making an issue of it.

Above: *Make the food on the plate more exciting to a child by creating a simple face that is easy to recognize.*

Below left: *A teddy bears' picnic may be a real treat. The child can feel in control and pretend to be a grown-up, and the novelty value should help the food go down quicker.*

Below right: *To make meals more exciting, try a different location occasionally, such as an indoor picnic on the floor.*

Left: *Be spontaneous about meals. On a warm summer evening take the table into the middle of the garden or find a sheltered corner. The children can carry everything outside and clear up.*

Right: *Roast chicken is easy to cook and will stretch if you have unexpected guests.*

Below: *Encourage the children to help with preparations. If they are keen cooks, ask them to make a pudding or decorate a pie for dessert.*

Family suppers

Supper can be a sacrosanct time in the life of a family. While each individual needs space and independence, a family also needs a focus, a time to come together as one unit on a regular basis. Supper is often the best time to do this. In fact, it may be the only time when the family comes together face to face. There is a great sense of wholeness and community when sitting around a table sharing food, conversation and laughter. The ideal environment for communication, it provides a good opportunity for children to learn the art of conversation and talking to adults.

The author Roald Dahl said that in his family 'we simply regard meals, and supper in particular, as a wonderful relaxing culmination to a day of hard work. Our suppers are times when work is forgotten and when food and wine are remembered.' Family supper should not be a time for lectures or stern words, but a time for relaxation and conviviality. It is a time to focus on positive things. Problems and pressing issues facing the family are better tackled in quiet moments before or after the meal. It is also a time for the children to put sibling rivalries and bad moods away and enjoy each other's company. And if the atmosphere is light-hearted, the children may well forget all about any fussy eating fads.

Getting youngsters to help prepare the meal is a good opportunity to teach them to serve others and to put other people's needs before their own. Ask them to get drinks for everybody, lay the table, help serve and clear away, and certainly to wash and dry up or load the dishwasher. Family supper could become quite a ritual, with each family member having their own tasks. Try not to differentiate the children's jobs between girls and boys – everyone can help! Delegate tasks according to age and ability. For older children, it may be an idea to alternate the tasks so that they do not quarrel about them. If washing and drying up becomes a real chore, try playing some of their favourite dance tracks to keep the mood fun.

As children grow up and flee the nest, it can be a nice family tradition to continue when they come back, especially if they bring friends or partners. Even if this doesn't happen very often, it still helps to keep the family bonds strong. Parents love to see their offspring gathered around a table.

'Father of all mankind, make the roof of my house wide enough for all opinions, oil the door of my house so it opens easily to friend and stranger and set such a table in my house that my whole family may speak kindly and freely around it.'

Hawaiian prayer

Family Playtime

From a spontaneous kick-around with a ball on a patch of grass, to industrious artwork or playing with family pets, leisure time can form the bedrock of many happy childhood memories.

If there is a corner of the home where the children can play undisturbed and make as much mess as they like, everyone will be much happier. A robust work surface and somewhere comfortable to relax will make the area much more versatile.

Making a playroom 118

Dressing up 126

Making music 130

Peace and quiet 132

Gardening 136

Family pets 142

Dens and hideaways 146

Nature trails 148

Barefoot living 150

Family Playtime

Leisure time is, of course, unique to every individual, and within a family each person will enjoy different activities in their spare time. Some children like football, Rollerblading or riding bikes, while others prefer playing with pets, working on computers or making things. The adults can be equally individual in their leisure pursuits, perhaps enjoying the cinema, walking in the countryside, gardening, decorating, reading or entertaining. What is significant about family leisure time, however, is that the activities are enjoyed together.

For children, leisure means a time when they are free to play. With so many demands being made on youngsters at school and in after-school activities, and television and computers taking up much of children's spare time, playing is a dying art. Yet play is vital in tapping into and developing children's vivid imaginations. Playtime is when they are in control – it is their own special world.

Playtime is also an opportunity for children to test their talents in the safe environment of the family. The budding actress unpacks the dressing-up box, the would-be veterinarian plays with the family pet, the future architect builds a shelter in the garden. What children remember about putting on a play at home or building a den is that they did it themselves. And, of course, they will remember the appreciative audience, the praise and the applause.

Surprisingly, family leisure time does not come easily. It doesn't always happen spontaneously but has to be worked at and planned carefully. Diaries have to be coordinated and time put aside in the calendar for these activities. Activities themselves may need planning, researching and booking, with a host of arrangements to be made.

If the family's diaries threaten to get so filled up that the benefits of leisure will themselves disappear, so include days in the diary – particularly at weekends – where nothing is planned. These create the opportunity for spontaneous, last-minute activities. So take some time out, put work to one side and enjoy simple pastimes together.

Making a playroom

Because there is often not enough time at school to spend on developing the creative arts, it is all the more important to encourage and make time for them outside of school. Not only do they develop children's skills at making things with their hands, but they also stimulate imagination and creativity. The activities do not have to involve a rigid timetable of events or extra classes to attend – they can easily be nurtured at home. In fact, the variety of creative activities that can be done at home is endless, from simple drawing and painting to multimedia and collage, or three-dimensional work and modelling. What is important is not to create a masterpiece but simply to enjoy the creative process itself.

The first step is to create an environment in which creative activities will spontaneously develop. The idea of making something is far more likely to occur to a child who isn't already fully occupied in watching television, so

'When I was their [children's] age, I could draw like Raphael, but it took me a lifetime to learn to draw like them.'

Pablo Picasso

reasonable rules about watching TV will have to be laid down and adhered to. Sometimes the projects children come up with can be fairly time-consuming, so the ideal time to organize them is at weekends or during school holidays.

An entire room need not be devoted to a playroom – the kitchen table will be perfectly adequate. Put together a box of potentially useful material and equipment, and add new items from time to time. Save cardboard boxes and old cereal packets for making models, yogurt pots for mixing paint, old wrapping paper and tissue paper as well as magazines and newspapers for collage, and scraps of fabric, ribbon, glittery milk bottle tops and colourful sweet wrappers. A box filled with this sort of treasure will inspire children to forget the television and start being creative.

In the summer, the creative work can be taken outdoors. Perhaps there is a garage or old shed, which may just need a couple of lights put in to make it a suitable room for children to play in. This is ideal because they can make

Below left: Be prepared for a lot of mess to clear up. Encourage the children to wear an old shirt or apron to protect their clothes from paint, as it is bound to get everywhere. Find a space to display all their work – it is a simple way to praise them.

Below: Flowerpots make good storage containers for art material. Large ones will hold all the paper and prevent it from getting creased, while small ones are ideal for brushes and pens. To make the flowerpots more decorative, children could paint them in different shades of emulsion paint.

Below right: It is a good idea to have somewhere to store the art materials, which must be kept out of a toddler's reach.

as much mess as they like. Turn the room into a studio. Create a wall for murals, whitewashing it so the children can paint on it. When the wall is full or too messy, whitewash it once more to create a fresh canvas. You could also use the garden as an outdoor studio.

If you do have a playroom, then more permanent equipment can be set up. A table is essential, such as an old garden or trestle table – you can cover it with a plastic cloth for permanent protection from paint spillages. Easels are ideal to paint at, as children can stand up instead of bending over a table. Have some old shirts or large aprons handy to protect their clothes. Good storage space is invaluable here. An old cupboard would be ideal for storing various art materials, and the children could each be given a drawer or a folder or 'portfolio' to keep all their latest work in. Buckets or dustbins are useful for storing rolls of paper if there is nowhere they can be stored flat. If you want to jazz up the playroom, try painting old pieces of junk furniture in luscious, contrasting colours. Make space for a large pinboard to display all the handiwork.

A large dustbin is essential for quick clearing up at the end, as creative play involves a lot of mess. It is important to be relaxed about the chaos – leave children to make the mess and wait until they really have finished before clearing up, even if the kitchen is taken over for the entire day. It's very tempting to follow children around, tidying up behind them, but this is very inhibiting to them.

These activities are great for involving others: parents, grandparents or friends can all join in. However, siblings or other relatives can easily undermine the first tentative attempts at creativity without realizing, so encouragement and enthusiasm are vital. The finished works of art should be treasured and valued, kept in a special place, hung on a wall, framed or photographed. Children may even want to hold an 'exhibition' of their latest work and invite friends and relatives to view it.

Far left (top to bottom): *Gentle guidance and encouragement from an adult will help give children confidence in their creative abilities. They may need to be taught the basics, such as how best to hold and use a paintbrush, draw a straight line and mix colours.*

Left: *A trolley (cart) is an ideal place to store art materials as it is so quick to put away.*

making a blackboard

You will need a piece of MDF (medium-density fibreboard) that has been cut to the size required, plus a pot of blackboard paint and a decorator's paintbrush. All these items are available from any good hardware store. Simply paint two coats of blackboard paint onto the wood, leaving it to dry between coats. Blackboard paint can also be applied to a flat cupboard door or directly to the wall. Mark out the area first with a pencil and a ruler.

Below and right: *Drawing on a blackboard is ideal for children because they can rub their drawing out if they make a mistake. Also, the large expanse encourages bold, free work.*

painting t-shirts

As far as children are concerned, the best way to display their handiwork is to wear it. Use clean white T-shirts that have been pre-washed and special fabric paints (available from good art shops).

❥ Decide which paint colours are going to be used – to be effective, only a few are needed. Suggest that the children plan their design first, perhaps sketching it on a sheet of paper, before starting to paint.

❥ Protect the surface with paper, and lay the T-shirt out flat on it. Put some layers of newspaper or plastic inside the T-shirt so the paint does not seep through from the front to the back of the T-shirt.

❥ Put all the paint in easy-to-use containers that will not fall over. Fabric paint may need to be diluted first so that it can be applied smoothly.

❥ Help the child to paint the design on the T-shirt. Younger children will need supervising and probably also will need help with the design. You could perhaps draw the outline for them and then they could colour it in.

❥ Leave the T-shirt to dry for several hours. Fix the colours if necessary (refer to the manufacturer's instructions). It should not be washed for at least four days, and then only in cold water.

Right and below: *Painting their own T-shirts is a great project for the whole family on a rainy day, holiday or weekend, and the results are bound to become the children's pride and joy. Painted T-shirts make great gifts, too.*

making a fairy doll

This delicate wire figure is very easy to make, and is light enough to hang from the ceiling with a double strand of thread.

❥ Mould lengths of thin wire into the basic form of the figure or animal. A rough outline is all that is needed, but the children will probably need an adult's help with this.

❥ Tear tissue paper into strips, paint the strips on one side with PVA glue (white glue), and wrap them around the figure like an Egyptian mummy. Leave the figure somewhere warm to dry overnight.

❥ Decorate the figure with paint or a material such as fabric, paper, string or ribbon. This woodland fairy's skirt was made from soft hand-made paper and the bodice and head-dress from pressed leaves and flowers.

❥ Handle the figure with care as it is very delicate. Thread a length of cotton thread through the top to provide a hanging loop.

screen-printing

In screen printing, paint is forced through a taut fabric screen onto the cloth being printed. Single-colour printing with simple motifs is easiest for children but they will need supervision. Use special screen-printing paints, a screen stretched over a frame and a squeegee (available from art shops) and pre-washed and ironed white calico to print on. The printed fabric is ideal for a cushion, curtain or shoe bag for school.

❥ Draw a simple silhouette shape on paper and cut it out. Cover the table with an old blanket and a piece of oilcloth or PVC fabric. Stretch a piece of white calico across the table and pin or tape it down.

❥ Lay the paper shape on a bottom corner of the calico and carefully place the screen on top. While someone else holds the frame, spoon some paint across one short end of the screen and spread it evenly across the screen with a squeegee. Carefully lift the screen from the fabric, without smudging, to reveal the printed image (the paper shapes will be 'glued' to the base of the screen by the paint).

❥ Place the screen alongside the first print and repeat the process to print a second image. Print enough fabric in this way for your required use. Fix the colours according to the manufacturer's instructions.

Dressing up

Dressing up is instinctive for children – they do it spontaneously, inspired by their vivid imaginations. Playing 'dressing up' is often the game that children enjoy before they start putting on plays. No rehearsing or planning is necessary, so the joy is instant. The simple pleasure of wearing fancy dress or an outrageous costume is something most children never outgrow.

The basic requirement is to have a dressing-up box. It does not have to be a fancy trunk – an old suitcase will do perfectly well. If specific clothes are put aside for dressing up, it will stop the children from raiding their parents' wardrobe for costumes quite so often. Dressing-up clothes do not need to be expensive costumes: simple cast-offs make highly original outfits. Old night-dresses and pyjamas are fun, particularly if accessorized with scarves

or shawls and perhaps a feather boa. The brighter and more exotic the clothing is, the better. There is nothing like an out-of-date piece of once-fashionable clothing, such as a puffball skirt or an old disco shirt, to create a fantastic costume. Don't let relatives throw away any old uniforms or evening dresses. If supplies or cast-offs from the family are low, stock up at the local charity shop or a jumble sale (rummage sale).

Donning a hat is the quickest way of changing identity, so it is a good idea to have lots of different hats, helmets, caps, crowns and tiaras, and perhaps also a jewellery box filled with securely strung colourful cheap beads. Sashes and ties are useful, because if the clothing is too big, the children can easily tie it up so that they can at least move in it without tripping over or the clothes falling off. Old shoes are popular and young girls will particularly enjoy tottering around in their mothers' old stilettos or platforms!

If the child is obsessed by one character, like a princess or Robin Hood, you could make a particular accessory to complete their costume – perhaps a gold tiara, or a cardboard shield and sword. If you 'construct' the chosen item, the child can then paint or decorate it themselves. Even something as simple as tying a bow on an old shower cap can create the ideal finishing touch to a princess costume.

Fabric remnants always make fantastic capes and shawls, especially if they are opulent material such as Lurex, brocade, velvet or lace, and old sheets or net curtains can be used to make wedding veils. Children also love to experiment with make-up. Simple face paints will complete a character's costume, or they could use an old lipstick. Girls love to put bright lipstick on 'just like Mummy'.

Putting on a play

Children are blessed with vivid imaginations, and putting on a play is a wonderful outlet for them. It can build their confidence, helping to counter-act the self-consciousness children often become prone to as they get older. And it gives them their first experiences of theatre, engendering an early love of drama which can last throughout their lives. Amateur dramatics in the home can involve children of all ages, as it isn't hard to find a part for even the youngest toddler. The play might be an extensive project, rehearsed over an entire weekend, or a spontaneous ten-minute performance which has taken only an hour to put together. As long as the audience is appreciative, with lots of clapping and shouts of 'encore!', children will discover for themselves the sheer magic of the theatre in their own home.

'Acting is not a profession for adults.'
Laurence Olivier

Far left and left above:
Essential for dressing up, hats are the quickest way of changing character.

Far left and left below:
Dressing up is a wonderful outlet for a child's imagination. They can dress up as their heroes and make their favourite stories come alive.

Right and far right above: Fill an old suitcase, box or trunk with a variety of cast-off clothes. Children will be able to put together a costume from anything.

Right below:
Specialized costumes such as animals may need some help from a parent, but they needn't be elaborate.

Although the children may need some help, try to let all the ideas come from them. A play can be inspired by anything, including storybooks, movies, television programmes, cartoon characters or favourite songs. It is easier to act without a script and just improvise if the story is familiar. Traditional fairy tales are ideal for this, as are fables and religious stories. As children get older, simple stories can be adapted to their own themes – for example, Little Red Riding Hood could be adapted so that she is a favourite pop star.

If the children are not so keen on performing, they could make a radio programme, recorded on a simple cassette player. As digital equipment becomes more sophisticated, it will not be long before youngsters make their own movies at home and show them on a video recorder. Musicals, pop concerts, talent shows, circus acts or fashion shows can all be wonderful to act and perform – children needn't restrict themselves just to a straight play. Some children may even act out the 'commercial breaks'.

Help the children to find a suitable spot to perform the play. Perhaps there is a room where curtains can be strung up. The living room floor makes a good stage, principally because adults can make themselves comfortable on the sofa and armchairs. If children are worried that it isn't a proper stage, explain that this is how theatre in the round is performed. Behind the sofa provides an excellent place for the children to hide before they are 'on stage', as well as an ideal place to change costume or hide props.

It might be an idea to make a props cupboard so children can feel really professional. Fill it with instruments, wands, plastic or cardboard swords and shields, a pair of wings, walking sticks, umbrellas and any other unusual bits and pieces that might come in handy. You could perhaps include some masks, too. If children are at a loss for ideas for a play, a visit to the props cupboard could be the starting point for a great idea.

tickets & programmes

To make the performance seem professional, like at a real theatre, encourage the children to make their own programmes and tickets.

Far left: *Sheets fastened to banisters with rubber bands make ideal theatre or stage curtains.*

Right: *If children insist on a 'proper' stage, raised above the audience, a spacious half-landing will do the trick. Otherwise, encourage them to put on their play 'in the round', surrounded by an audience at the same level as the performers.*

Below: *Children's theatrical experiments may lead them to discover for themselves dramatic effects such as backlighting, created by sunshine.*

Making music

To teach a child to love and appreciate music is to give them a gift they will have for life. Playing an instrument isn't necessary for the enjoyment of music, as humans have an inbuilt instrument – the voice. Singing is an invaluable skill for a child to develop, as they can sing anywhere and anytime, either alone or with others.

Many schools these days encourage children to learn an instrument and to play in a school band or orchestra. Learning to play music is excellent for a child, even if they don't persevere with it to an advanced level. No matter how rudimentary their efforts, they will immediately get an enormous satisfaction from mastering a simple tune. As they progress, they will get more and more pleasure from playing. In addition, learning about rhythm, harmony and melody, as well as learning to read music, is of enormous value. And, as with acting in amateur dramatics, playing an instrument in front of an audience is very good for building a child's confidence.

Music lessons will almost certainly be required to nurture a particular interest in an instrument, but unless the child has a particular gift for music, the priority should be simply to ensure that they enjoy their lessons. That doesn't mean, however, that they can be allowed to practise only when the mood takes them, as they'd be unlikely ever to progress. The next time you wonder whether all the nagging is really worth it, remember that even child prodigies sometimes have to be forced to practise! And when a child does actually start practising without being told to, give them some praise.

Children will need plenty of support to help them persevere, so don't send them away to a quiet room for their practice – encourage them to do it somewhere they can be heard and you can let them know how good it is (even if they sound absolutely awful, as they probably will early on). Keep their instrument in a room where all the family gathers together. Special music rooms sound a good idea, but unless they are used for other purposes as well, or the family is extremely musical, they can be too isolated. Keeping musical instruments, music stands and sheet music close at hand will encourage more spontaneous sessions.

Once a piece of music has been learnt, it can be enjoyed for a lifetime. Childhood tunes rarely disappear from memory. The music doesn't have to be complicated to give pleasure – simple pieces such as chopsticks can be played over and over by children (and usually are, as long-suffering parents know all too well). Nor do music lessons have to revolve around classical

Left: Encourage interest in all styles of music. Popular songs and jazzy tunes may be easier for a young child to appreciate than a classical piece.

Below: Whatever the time of day and wherever children practise, whether it's at a portable music stand or at a piano, make sure they have good light for reading the music.

pieces. Children may find popular music and jazz easier to appreciate. Either find a music teacher who can teach a wide variety of musical styles to retain the child's interest, or, if the teacher insists on classical musical (as many do), supplement this with fun pieces the child can play in their spare time. Music stores sell a wide range of sheet music for all instruments.

Music is rewarding both as a solo activity and as part of a group. To accompany singers on the piano or to be part of a band or orchestra is particularly good fun, not only for the pleasure of making music but also for the satisfaction of doing so as part of a team. Older children can suggest that friends who play the same instrument bring their instruments with them when they visit; you could possibly obtain some sheet music of a suitable level so that they can play duets. Siblings might also enjoy playing duets.

Even when children are quite young, they can be encouraged to play music together. Just banging a drum, shaking a tambourine or playing simple rhythms on a saucepan with a wooden spoon to an accompaniment is enough. Keep a box of children's instruments, such as a xylophone, drum, maracas, tambourine, triangle, woodblock, kazoo or recorder, and get younger children playing when they visit.

Persuade them to give a concert to the rest of the family. It is good for parents to be involved, too, whether singing along, playing instruments themselves or dancing to the music. Family jam sessions are great fun. Encourage brothers and sisters to play together, whether their instruments and skill levels are suited to this or not. Make sure that everyone has something to play, even if it's just an improvised percussion instrument. Musical talent is not a prerequisite – just enthusiasm.

Below left: *To help with learning the notes on the keyboard, write the names of the notes on sticky labels to put on the keys temporarily.*

Below centre: *Children need particular encouragement in the early stages of learning an instrument, when their fingers have not yet become nimble and everything is unfamiliar and difficult.*

Below right: *Children prefer to practise their instruments wherever the rest of the family is. Fortunately some instruments can be taken anywhere.*

Peace and quiet

Amongst the everyday hubbub of busy and demanding family life, everyone needs to find opportunities for some moments of peace and quiet, stillness and relaxation. Parents will probably relish those rare moments alone, either reading, listening to music or relaxing in a hot bath. Children need to learn to be happy with their own company and to amuse themselves. When a child is reading a book, for example, the television or radio should be turned off, to eliminate any possible distractions. If a parent is trying to listen to a piece of music or read a newspaper article, the children need to be taught not to interrupt them constantly.

Below left: *Find a warm, sunny spot in the house to be quiet for half an hour and concentrate on a good book. Story time is not just for bedtime.*

Below: *Make time in the day to stop and be still. Turn off the television or radio, and read a book. Encourage siblings to enjoy a book together – the older ones can read to the youngest.*

Below right: *Take time to look at old family photo albums, reminiscing and sharing stories. Children may particularly enjoy hearing stories from their grandparents about their own parents when they were children.*

Taking time out doesn't necessarily mean solitary activities. Reading aloud to a child, and getting them to read to you, not only is a good way to share a book and some quality time, but also helps develop the child's reading skills. This applies to older children as much as young ones; it's important for reading aloud not to stop just because a child has learned to read. Dig out family photograph albums and reminisce. With today's hectic lifestyles, this has become something of a luxury that most people never find time to enjoy, but family memories and history are very precious. Put some time aside in the winter months to keep family albums up to date. Compile a scrapbook and fill it with snippets of family history and a family tree. Photo albums and scrapbooks are often a family's most treasured possession.

'Community is always poised between two poles:
solitude and togetherness. Without togetherness
community disperses; without solitude community
collapses into a mass, a crowd.'

David Steindl-Rast

Below: *Playing games is a wonderful means of
building bridges between family members and
different generations.*

Family games

Games offer an excellent opportunity for a family to participate all together in something. Children love their parents or older siblings to be involved in their own games. Playing games is not only great entertainment but also assists in child development. Games can provide mental stimulation, teaching children how to concentrate. They also further emotional development, helping children learn how to deal with frustration, jealousy, disappointment, impatience, joy and pride.

Social skills are developed, too, because games teach them to get along with others, whether they are part of the same team or playing against one another. Competition is a fact of life and something children cannot avoid as they grow up, so learning how to handle it from a young age is invaluable. The ability to cooperate and work as a team is equally crucial, and sometimes difficult for children to learn, particularly if they have no siblings to have to cooperate with. The good thing about games is that they simultaneously develop both aspects – the ability to cooperate and the ability to handle competition – and give children opportunities to learn how to be good losers and magnanimous winners.

The games a family enjoys will depend on the ages and personalities of the children and will obviously change as they grow older and their interests develop. One child may become hooked on chess, while another, possibly more extrovert child may insist on playing charades. Expensive board games are not required for great entertainment. A pencil and paper offer a wide variety of exciting games, from consequences or noughts and crosses (tic-tac-toe) to hang-man or battleships.

Some games are wonderful played alone. The card game patience (solitaire), of which there are many variations, can keep a child amused for hours. A jigsaw puzzle is particularly good for developing visual skills, as well as concentration, and can be played with one or many people. There are a few classic two-player games, such as chess, backgammon, draughts (checkers) and Othello, that will be enjoyed for a lifetime.

Games involving the entire family are often memorable occasions, from twister and Monopoly to squeak-piggy-squeak and blind man's buff. Children love to see their parents behaving like children, acting out funny charades, for example, and joining in the fun wholeheartedly. Games as simple as hide-and-seek or sardines can amuse children for hours. The thrill of finding a secret hiding place is like discovering hidden treasure. There are also a host of word games and general-knowledge games, which can offer educational benefits as well as fun.

Card games can be played anywhere, on a train, at home or taken on holiday. A fast game like racing demon is great for getting the adrenalin going and developing quick reflexes, fast thinking and total concentration. Pelmanism, in which matching pairs are selected from cards laid face down, is an ideal memory exercise. Games like trumps involve more careful strategy skills. Whatever a family's favourites, all generations can enjoy playing card games together.

Below: The perennial appeal of card games stems from the fact that they fit in a pocket and can be used for a wide variety of games.

easy card games

Pelmanism: Shuffle the pack and lay all the cards out face down on a flat surface. Each player takes it in turn to turn over two cards, see what they are and turn them back again. It's a memory test, so the aim of the game is to make pairs of cards. When a player finds a pair, they take the pair out of play and retain them; they then have another go. At the end of the game, the winner is the player with the most pairs.

Snap: This is a game for two players. Shuffle the pack and divide it in two. Each player turns a card over on the table at the same time. When two identical cards are placed down at the same time, the players race to be the first to say 'snap'. The one who does so takes all the cards that have been put face up on the table. The players then continue to turn all the cards over and call 'snap'. The winner is the player who manages to win the entire pack of cards.

Gardening

Parents should not expect too much of children when they are gardening, as it is a very adult activity – just for them to be involved is often enough. Helping with simple jobs like digging holes in a flowerbed for planting bulbs and generally clearing up is a good place to start, since young children love making mud pies and getting messy.

Raking leaves is easy for all ages to do. Use short, light planks of wood to pick the leaves up; a child-sized rake would also make the job easier. Of course, half the fun of raking leaves is diving into the pile afterwards and throwing the leaves in the air, so you'll have to accept that enjoyment is the priority and actually clearing up the leaves comes second. Making a bonfire of leaves or other garden refuse is always enjoyable for children, but it must be closely supervised by a parent at all stages. Youngsters could help by collecting kindling for it.

The gardening activities a child enjoys will obviously depend on their age and personality. Watering is a task that all ages can help with, though younger children may need supervision when using a garden hose, to ensure that the plants are not overwatered. (Also, in baking-hot weather, playing in the water is likely to prove such an irresistible temptation that the plants will be forgotten completely.) A child-sized watering can is easier to carry than a large one, but will also require a lot of trips.

An older child may enjoy smartening up the edges of a lawn. Dead-heading is a job most children like (though it's not suitable for the very young, who shouldn't use sharp scissors or pruning shears on their own and who, at any rate, would probably happily dead-head every flower in sight). Pruning can be a satisfying activity for older children, but doing it properly is quite tricky and so it will require assistance and guidance.

This kind of garden maintenance is not only a genuine help to parents, but it also helps children to be aware of what is growing in their garden. You could encourage them to look out for unusual leaves and pretty flowers, which they could press between pieces of blotting paper in a flower press or under heavy books.

Some children regard helping a parent in the garden as another form of dutiful household chore – on a par with doing the dusting or vacuuming the floors – and are not very interested in becoming involved. However, a grandparent may have more success. The novelty for the child of being in a different place, with a grandparent who probably spoils them, could make

Top right: *Gardening is a good opportunity for children to learn to assist with domestic chores, and all generations can share in tasks like weeding and planting.*

Centre right: *Young children may surprise you with their enthusiasm and tenacity when gardening.*

Below: *Older children can prove really useful in the garden. Children of all ages usually enjoy helping when visiting grandparents.*

gardening more exciting. This can also be a good solution for busy parents who have little time to enjoy gardening with their children. Grandparents generally have much more time to spare and would probably love the help and companionship. It could also become a special activity for them to share, and may grow into a life-long interest.

Above: *Growing sunflowers is an enjoyable gardening project for children. They may need help initially, but once the seedlings are established, children can monitor the flowers' growth almost daily – it's exciting for them to measure their own height against that of the plant. Sunflowers are usually fairly easy to grow and the seeds can be saved and feed to the birds.*

'Children's children are a crown to the aged, and parents are the pride of their children.'

Proverbs

Growing plants

Growing things is what every child wants to do in the garden, and even if you have only a window box or balcony garden, it's possible for children of any age to do this. However, it is a more long-term project than people often realize. Waiting six to twelve weeks for seeds to grow can feel like a lifetime to a child. Therefore, start by giving the children seeds that grow quickly. Mustard and cress are the quickest to grow, with almost overnight success, and can also be grown indoors and at any time of year (see page 141).

Showy flowers and vegetables are easy for children to appreciate. Sweet peas or nasturtiums, for example, are colourful and prolific, while sunflowers are perhaps the showiest flowers of all, possibly even growing taller than the child. Although it takes time for sunflowers to sprout, they will grow quickly once they are well established, and children can enjoy measuring them each day. Encourage them to water the plant daily – a child-sized watering-can will make this easier, though you will probably have to supplement it. It might be fun also to plant a 'family tree' together and watch it get bigger as the children grow up.

If children are particularly enthusiastic and you have the space in your garden, you could give them their own plot. Get them to help you prepare the area by digging, weeding and adding some compost. If you don't have the space for a whole plot, giving the child a couple of their own large flowerpots, a window box or a growbag would be sufficient.

If growing plants still proves too difficult, harvesting is an ideal task for children as the results are instant. Collecting vegetables or picking fruit are very simple tasks. A 'pick-your-own' plot will suffice, or take a country walk in late summer and collect blackberries from the hedgerows.

Far right: Picking fruit or vegetables is a fun task for children to help with. It can be exciting delving among dense leaves to discover ripe fruit or berries and to taste a few before they go in the basket.

Right (top and bottom): Planting seeds in flowerpots and nurturing them over the weeks requires some patience, skill and help from an adult, but the satisfaction gained from watching the tiny seedlings develop is enormous.

'See! The winter is past, the rain is over and gone. The flowers appear on the earth; the season of singing has come, and the voice of the turtle dove is heard in our land.'

Song of Songs

To sow seeds, prepare the ground and water it the day before. Allow the child to scatter the seeds over the ground. Rake them into the soil so they are just buried. In dry weather, water them two days after sowing, and then a week after that. When the seedlings have two or three true leaves, thin them out.

Bulbs are some of the easiest plants for children to grow and can be grown in either the ground or in window boxes. The bulbs themselves are more impressive then tiny seeds, and it is more fun for a child to dig a hole and bury a bulb than to scatter a handful of seeds. If a colourful label is set into the ground with the bulbs, the child has something to look at while the weeks tick by and you wait for them to appear. Bear in mind that there will be less of a wait for summer- and autumn-flowering bulbs, which are planted in spring and summer respectively, than for spring-flowering bulbs, which are planted the previous autumn. On the other hand, it's hard to beat the excitement of seeing the first flowers of the year, snowdrops, which are planted in early autumn or, even earlier, after flowering.

Different bulbs have different planting and flowering times. Most prefer a sunny site, though a few, such as snowdrops and cyclamen, like partially shaded sites. The basics of planting bulbs are very simple. Prepare the ground first by digging, weeding and adding some compost or peat, then, using a dibber (dibble) or a trowel, dig a hole about twice as deep as the bulb. Pop the bulb down the hole, with the point or bud pointing upwards, and cover over with soil. Water the spot if the soil gets too dry, depending on the amount of rainfall.

Right: Children find it hard to imagine that a handful of hard, round bulbs can grow into beautiful, delicate flowers.

Far right: Allow children to be involved in each step of planting bulbs, from digging the hole and putting in the bulb, to carefully filling in with soil and finally labelling the spot with a home-made plant label. They expect to see a plant growing within days, so you will have to explain the need for patience.

'Flowers of all hue, and without thorn the rose.'
John Milton

making plant labels

If children are planting lots of seeds and bulbs, these hand-made labels will help them remember what went where as they await the flowers' appearance. Use some sticky-backed plastic to protect the labels from rain and straight twigs to stick them in the ground (see right for the finished label in use).

❧ *Cut out the label from white card. Paint or draw on it a picture of what the plant will look like. You may want to include the name of the plant. Stick the picture on a slightly bigger piece of coloured card, to create a nice frame.*

❧ *Cut one piece of clear sticky-backed plastic that is the same shape but slightly bigger than the label. Cut a second that is the mirror image of this. Peel the backing off the first piece of plastic and carefully stick it on the front of the label. Stick the other piece on the back in the same way. Trim the edges with scissors so that the plastic extends just slightly beyond the edges of the label. This is important to stop it from getting ruined by rain.*

❧ *Make a hole in the top and bottom of the label with a hole punch. If the twig is thick you may need to make the hole slightly bigger with a pencil. Slot the twig through from front to back, and then out to the front again through the other hole. Stick it in the ground next to where the seeds or bulbs have been planted.*

growing mustard and cress

These are simplicity itself to grow. They can be grown in soil in pots decorated with faces, but they don't really even need soil and can be grown on blotting paper, which makes it all seem rather like magic. Growing them is all the more satisfying because they can be eaten at the end of the process.

❧ Paint a face on a small flowerpot or draw one on a paper or polystyrene cup, and fill the pot with soil. Alternatively, simply dampen some blotting paper and lay it on a plate. Sprinkle mustard and cress seeds lightly on top of the soil or paper.

❧ Place the pot or plate in a warm place such as an airing cupboard, and keep the soil or blotting paper moist. The seeds should sprout within a few days.

❧ When they are about 8cm (3in) tall, trim off the sprouts, wash, dry and add to salads or to egg-salad sandwiches.

Family pets

Children feel a special affinity for animals which is both instinctive and deep-rooted. Whether they are flinging their arms around a dog or cuddling a hamster, they tend to shower their pets with affection. At times the animals will be talked to like humans, and at other times treated like live toys. If a child has been told off or is upset, solace can be found in having a hug with the family pet – the warm body and soft fur provide comforting reassurance. Indeed, a pet offers the whole family an outlet for much love and affection. Bonds between animals and their owners can sometimes seem almost as strong as those between humans, and adults remember their childhood pets with great affection.

Even so, it can be a big decision whether or not to have a family pet. Like children, they need feeding, cleaning, exercising and generally looking after. With some pets, such as ponies, this can be extremely expensive and time-consuming. In addition, pets that live in the home may leave hairs everywhere, make the house and car smell, ruin the furniture by chewing or sharpening their claws on it, cause allergies, make noise and bring in animals they've caught. It can be complicated if the family wants to go away and the pet cannot accompany them, and pets can be expensive in terms of vets' bills and kennel costs as well as food. Yet despite this catalogue of potential problems, they are still enormously, and deservedly, popular. Because a pet

Left (top and bottom): Cats can be quite independent, needing their own space and going their own way. However, they are less work to look after than a dog and are often good companions.

Below left: A rabbit is delightfully soft and furry but needs an enclosed area to run around in.

Below: Gerbils and hamsters are easy to have in the home because they stay all the time in their cages – apart from the occasional escape.

is part of the family, and in particular means so much to the children, many people are prepared to put up with the drawbacks.

Having pets of their own teaches children to be responsible for others besides themselves, but adults should still be prepared to do most of the work involved in looking after the pet. Start by giving children small tasks, feeding being the obvious one. Suggest that the pet be fed before children have their own meal. Some animals also need regular exercising, and older children should do their share of this. In order to prevent a pet from dominating the home and family life, a few rules may have to be laid down. For example, perhaps the animal will be allowed only into certain rooms or not be allowed on the furniture.

Living in a town obviously limits the type of pet a family can have. Dogs, cats, fish and small creatures that live in huts or cages are the most common pets in towns. Dogs tend to be great companions and the most loyal of friends, but their characters vary greatly and some are more child-friendly than others. Some dogs may be too aggressive to have around children.

'Some of my best leading men have been dogs and horses.'

Elizabeth Taylor

Right and below: *Puppies are a lot of work to look after, but they do offer huge rewards in love and entertainment – and are, of course, irresistible.*

Below left: *Dogs are often children's best friends. They will follow their owners around the house and are always ready to play games.*

Left: *Loyal and devoted companions, dogs may want to be involved in every activity their family enjoys.*

Right: *Birds can easily be attracted into the garden with a bird table or seed holder. Put it near a window so the birds can be viewed from inside the house.*

Cats are generally more aloof than dogs. Although many are tolerant of children, others can sometimes be so independent that nobody can get close to them. Thus, the advantage of a cat being able to exercise itself, coming and going through its catflap, may be outweighed by the children's frustration in not being able to bestow their affection on their pet. A friendly, lovable dog or cat can, however, become a lifelong friend.

Fish are worth getting only if they can be given a lovely large tank, full of greenery, and another fish or two as companions. A bowl of murky water containing a lone fish neither sets a good example to the child nor makes for a good life for the fish. Birds can also be difficult animals to keep cooped up in cages; only certain birds, such as parrots, are easy to interact with, and they tend to be allowed free access to the house.

Rabbits, guinea pigs, hamsters and gerbils have the advantage of being furry, small and portable. They need regular handling and the odd run in an enclosed space, otherwise their life is too cooped up. They are not affectionate, however, and they have a short life expectancy, which can be traumatic to a child. Also, hamsters and gerbils are nocturnal, so they are generally asleep when the children are awake and vice-versa.

Living in the countryside extends the range of possible pets, adding horses, chickens, goats, ducks, sheep, perhaps even a cow to the list. Farm animals can be very rewarding. Not only might they provide organic eggs or milk for breakfast, but they will also help a child appreciate where food comes from. A child may learn a lot more from seeing hens raise their chicks, or from helping to care for a newborn lamb, than from clearing out a gerbil cage.

Think carefully before you buy a pony or horse. It can take over the family's entire life, so make sure that is what you want. It will need more care and attention than any other animal; therefore, time, money and your level of commitment are vital factors to consider. Feeding, mucking out, grooming and cleaning tack are all necessary on a more-or-less daily basis, and the pony or horse has to be exercised frequently, regardless of the weather. In addition, children are likely to become involved in riding classes and gymkhanas or horse shows, all of which demand further time. Owning a horse or pony is a wonderful source of pleasure and relaxation, provided you are prepared for your family to spend every spare minute with it.

'Dear God, please make me the kind of person my dog thinks I am.'

Anonymous

Above left: *Animals provide companionship for each other, often proving almost inseparable.*

Below left: *Geese are excellent at sentry duty, announcing every visitor with their loud, honking cries, and sometimes proving quite aggressive.*

Below: *Some people keep goats for their milk, which is more easily digested than cows' milk. Goats have lots of personality and can even be walked in the same way as dogs.*

Dens and hideaways

The world of fantasy is often very real to children, and building a den or hideaway of their own is a superb means of expression for their vivid imaginations. A den is a place exclusively for children. Perhaps a friend, a teddy or a pet may be invited in, but otherwise it is their own secret world, where they are in charge. The construction of the den is, of course, great fun in itself, but playing inside is its raison d'être. A den is a safe haven, a place of security, which taps into the basic nesting instinct. It is a way of 'playing house'. Many a child's den will have provisions, either real or pretend, and there may also be chairs, a table and even a bed.

Dens are hugely varied but creating one is very simple. All that is needed is a selection of fabric remnants, rugs or bedspreads plus a little imagination. Dens can be outdoors, for example under trees or behind a shed, or indoors, such as under the stairs or under a table with a cloth over it. The sofa can be a ship to dive from and discover buried treasure; the bed might be a desert island.

Above left: *A den provides a base from which children can go on adventures – it is the base camp of their imaginative world.*

Far left: *Anywhere private, even an old shed, is suitable for a den. It might have a cash register, for selling goodies to a select clientele of pets or special friends.*

Left and right: *A barn provides a perfect hideaway for children as well as chickens. Here a simple child-scale home has been set up, for playing house.*

Nature trails

Nature trails and treasure hunts are outdoor activities that most children can easily join in, including children who are not keen on sport. Combining exercise and fresh air with intellectual challenges and teamwork, they are great ways of turning simple walks into games or adventures.

Treasure hunts can be sophisticated enough for adults as well as children to participate in, but these need careful planning, with elaborate clues, puzzles and maps to follow. It's much easier to begin with a simpler version like a scavenger hunt, which turns the observation of nature into a game. Give the children a list of simple objects to hunt for (see checklist below) and a bag to put their discoveries in. Older children could be given more difficult things to find, and all the children could perhaps be divided into teams, to turn it into a race. Whoever designs the scavenger hunt may have to scout the area first for ideas on what to look for. Apart from the thrill of discovering the treasures, scavenger hunts encourage an observant eye and help teach children to value the beautiful treasures found in nature. Something as simple as a feather found in the woods or a shell collected on a beach can become a cherished possession.

Another exciting game requiring lots of running around involves following a nature trail through the woods. One person, or a group, sets off in advance and leaves a trail of clues behind them. They may need quite a good head start – at least twenty minutes or so. Clues can include a pile of rocks or an arrow chalked on a tree or stone. You could even think up rhyming clues. A red-herring trail can be left, too, with a cross at the end of the path to show that they have to go back. An advanced version of this is 'hare and hounds', in which all the hares run off to hide, leaving false trails, and the hounds have to chase and find them. But no matter how simple or complex the nature trail, it is a fun way of encouraging children to enjoy the natural world.

checklist for a scavenger hunt

green leaf	blue flower
yellow leaf	yellow flower
prickly leaf	moss
smooth stone	piece of bark
pink stone	fork-shaped twig
feather	glittery pebble
fir cone	snail shell

Opposite page: *Use a piece of chalk to lay a trail through the woods. Also make arrows in the ground with twigs.*

This page: *Make a nature table at home where all the treasures of the scavenger hunt can be kept. Use different containers for different things – feathers, leaves, shells, nuts and so on.*

Barefoot living

To a child, the beach is a gigantic adventure playground. There are waves to chase and jump over, sandcastles to build, rock pools containing hidden treasure to discover, and endless games to play barefoot on soft sand. A day at the beach is perhaps the ultimate family excursion, as it has something to offer everyone, from babies experiencing sand for the first time, to grandparents dozing on a deckchair. As a place to play a ball game, throw a frisbee, fly a kite or run around just for the sheer pleasure of it, a sandy beach is unbeatable. The vast expanses of sand, sky and sea give a sense of freedom found nowhere else, the air is invigorating and at any time you can cool off in the water. (In some seas, this is possible after just sticking one toe in the water.) A picnic never tastes as good as when there's sand in the sandwiches, and afterwards the warm sand provides the perfect place to lie down and sunbathe, snooze or read.

As if all this were not enough, sand is remarkably child-friendly, being nice to handle, easy to run on (at least on the damp part) and soft to fall on. Although adults tend to get preoccupied by practicalities at the beach, such as how to get

Below: *A sandy beach is the perfect playground for children. The sand is a lovely surface on which to run and jump, as well as a great material for creative play.*

Right and below right: *Running in and out of the breaking waves, chasing them up and down the beach to the sound of the crashing surf, never loses its thrill.*

the windbreak to stay up or whether to put on more sunscreen, children have a much more elemental response. They instinctively realize that here is a place where they can feel wild and free, liberated from society's restraints. One day by the sea can be like a whole holiday in the mind of a child, creating enough happy memories to last a lifetime.

A trip to the beach doesn't have to involve an entire holiday or weekend. If you don't live too many hours from the sea, it's simple enough to fill a basket with swimsuits, towels and a picnic, jump in the car or on a bus or train, and head off to the sea just for the day. To a child, a day at the beach can seem like three days rolled into one, as all the experiences are so vivid. In fact, the simple pleasures of a day at the seaside will restore anyone, whether they are nine or ninety.

*'We had sand in the eyes and the ear and the nose,
and sand in the hair, and sand between the toes.'*

A A Milne

Kite flying

Flying kites is a popular pastime for adults and children alike. The beach is an ideal place for kite flying, as there is almost always a good breeze blowing offshore. Hours can be spent playing with the wind, making the kite duck and dive around the sky. Kites come in a huge variety of shapes, including boxes, pyramids, fish and dragons, but the easiest kite for beginners to fly is probably the simple 'keel-guided', or 'delta', kite, which is both inexpensive and widely available. However, making your own kite is part of the fun (see right), and the simplest type to make is the traditional flat, diamond-shaped kite with a tail for balance.

Flying a kite is not as easy as it looks, so be prepared to provide a lot of help if necessary. A large kite is easier to fly than a small one, but it shouldn't be so large that a child can't manage it. The best wind for kite flying is a good, steady breeze.

'Let's go fly a kite – up to the highest height'
Mary Poppins

Right and below: *To fly a kite, stand with your back to the wind and hold the kite up. (Or if a child wants to run into the wind while holding the kite up, this usually works, too.) When the wind catches it and takes it up into the air, slowly let out the cord, occasionally tugging on it to make it climb higher. Paying out the cord will make it descend. If the kite starts to dive, however, you need to pay out some cord to allow it to swing around into an upright position again.*

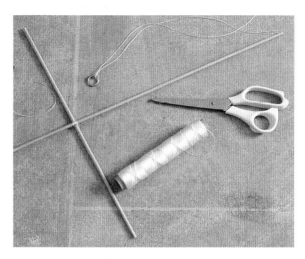
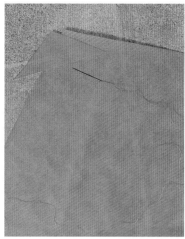
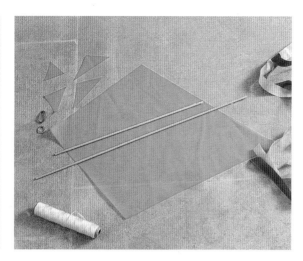

making a kite

Use special kite fabric, wooden dowelling and nylon thread to make this traditional, diamond-shaped kite. The materials are available from kite shops and large haberdashers (notions stores).

❥ Make a template out of newspaper; this kite was about 50 x 30cm (20 x 12in). Using the template, cut the main kite shape out of kite fabric. Also cut out four small triangles to fit each corner.

❥ Sew the triangles to the corners of the kite, sewing only along the two outer edges to create pockets to hold the dowelling.

❥ Using the template as a guide to size, cut two lengths of wooden dowelling to fit the width and depth of the kite. Form the dowels into a cross, and bind together securely. Cut a 70cm (28in) length of nylon thread, fold it in half, push the loop through a small metal curtain ring and then pull the two ends of the thread through the loop, leaving the ring at the centre of the thread.

❥ Slot the dowels into the corners, then sew two long, narrow strips of kite material or coloured plastic to the bottom.

❥ Wrap a very long length of nylon thread around a twig or kite handle, tying the other end to the metal ring. Make two tiny holes in the kite, insert the two free ends of the nylon thread through the kite from the front, and attach them to the longer dowel as shown.

Sandcastles and beachcombing

Beachcombers were originally people who lived off the flotsam and jetsam on the seashore, and there are still so many treasures to be found washed up by the sea that we can all be beachcombers for a day. Many pleasurable hours can be spent walking up and down the beach, trailing feet in the lapping waves, looking for beautiful pebbles, shells and pieces of driftwood. These make perfect souvenirs of a holiday and look nice at home stored in jars, decorating items or simply used as paperweights, doorstops or sculptures in their own right.

Of course, the childhood pastime most closely associated with the beach is building sandcastles. Sand offers a wealth of diverse creative possibilities, and consequently sandcastles remain just as popular with every succeeding generation. Complete beginners can start with simple castles. Fill a bucket with damp sand (trial and error will reveal how damp it needs to be), turn it upside down so the sand comes out in one piece and decorate the castle with shells or pebbles. Dig a moat all around it and either fill the moat with water brought in buckets from the sea, or wait for a wave to come in and turn

Below left: The creative possibilities for sandcastle building on a beach are huge. The castles can be small or large – a child could build a whole village of small sandcastles surrounded by a wall, or one giant castle with many turrets.

Below: The beach is full of decorative objects to adorn the sandcastles, from shells and stones to feathers, seaweed and seaside flowers.

it into an island. Once this is mastered, the sky is the limit and all manner of elaborate castles with moats and drawbridges are possible.

Sand art is another creative venture that is perennially popular. Bury a willing volunteer in the sand with just their head poking up, and give them a new body constructed from damp sand. Enlist the help of the whole family to build a large dragon decorated with pebbles and shells, or perhaps a car with a seat where the children can sit and pretend to drive. Make a beautiful mermaid reclining on the sand and decorate her tail and her hair with fronds of seaweed collected from the shoreline.

Below: Create a seaside mobile to remind the family of happy days at the beach. Cut out lots of seaside motifs from card, and thread them on string or cotton along with bits of shells or driftwood. Attach to a coathanger or old lampshade frame to hang it up.

Below right: Collect pebbles and pieces of driftwood and shingle to complete a seaside collection of flotsam and jetsam.

Far right (top and bottom): Collecting shells is a wonderful natural treasure hunt. This is one pastime that few people outgrow.

'What a blessing is the childish nature which clothes dull surroundings in fancy dress and drives dull cares away. The sand pile where we played after the red sun went down was transformed into moats and castles with just as much enjoyment as if the land, like Canaan, had been flowing with milk and honey.'

Anonymous nineteenth-century female pioneer

Rainy days

Of course, it is not always sunny and warm at the beach. The challenge is to amuse a family at the beach on a cold, grey day when it is drizzling or even pouring with rain. One option is simply to defy the weather, dressing up in warm waterproof clothes and boots and going for an invigorating walk on the beach. Play games like catch or grandmother's footsteps, which involve lots of running so that nobody gets cold or notices the rain running down their neck. Even if it is only a short walk, at least everyone will have got some sea air. While walking, encourage the children to watch for footprints in the sand – from dogs, horses, birds, people – and invent stories to go with the prints. Explore rock pools at low tide – the children are likely to become so absorbed that they forget the rain. Be sure to show them how to handle the creatures they find there very carefully, and to put them back where they found them afterwards.

You may have to eat your picnic in the car and perhaps listen to a good story tape or music, make up silly games or sing songs. At the very least, it will have been a memorable day.

If you are staying in a house at the beach, bring out the treasures you have collected from beachcombing, and let everyone admire them. Stand at the window and scan the beach and any cliffs for bird life. At the beach house or when you return home, create some fun activities inspired by the beach. Decorate a box or picture frame with shells. Put pebbles in a vase of water to bring out the patterns and colours. Start collecting different kinds of sand collected from the beaches you visit, displaying them in a wooden box with sections, or in large matchboxes glued together to form a cardboard display box. Paint some seaside pictures. Make some giant colourful fish with a paper collage – or be inspired by the ideas on this page.

Below left and right:
On a rainy day, find creative activities that are inspired by the seaside. Paint paper boats in summery colours, decorate a picture frame with shells or paint pictures of beach life.

Below: Don't let bad weather deter you from enjoying the beach. Just find a sheltered spot to get warm afterwards.

pebble dominoes

This should keep children occupied for at least part of a long rainy day, particularly if they spend some time collecting the pebbles at the seaside first. You will need at least 36 smooth pebbles of a similar shape and size for a good game of dominoes. To add the domino markings, use either a black marker pen or a paintbrush and enamel paint.

❧ *Give the pebbles a quick wash to remove any sand, and put some newspaper or plastic sheeting down to protect the work surface.*

❧ *Draw or paint a line across the middle of each pebble, then add any number of dots from one to six on each side of the line. Make sure all the dominoes are different and that every combination is included. Some dominoes will be 'doubles', with the same number on both sides. Leave the paint to dry before you play.*

❧ *To play, divide the domino pebbles evenly between all the players. Each person takes it in turn to put a domino down, with one half matching the previous domino, as shown. The winner is the first person to use up all their dominoes.*

index

Acknowledgments

The author would like to thank all those at Collins & Brown: to Kate Kirby for understanding the vision and giving me a wonderful opportunity; to Gillian Haslam for her patience, support and encouragement; to Christine Wood for beautiful layouts and art direction; and to Alison Wormleighton for editing my chaotic text. A big thank you to Jacqui Hurst for her wonderful eye, for such energy and enthusiasm on the shoots, and capturing the vision in her photographs. Unending thanks to my parents, John and Kate Dyson, without whom I would not know the joys of family life. Most of all, thank you to my husband, Titus, for support, inspiration and just about everything, and to J.C. for amazing grace.

The author and publisher would like to thank the families who kindly allowed us to photograph them and their homes: Vanessa and Nicholas Arbuthnott, George, Rose, Flora and Edmund; Natasha Beattie and Chantelle; Minna and Peveril Bruce, Otto, Finn and Todd; Kate and John Dyson; Sue and David Elton, Octavia and Theo; Suzanne Faure and Sapphire; Tako Jabang and Kai; Anke and Brian Ma Siy and Nicholas; Ros and Neil Mills; Mark and Dana Mills-Powell, Bridget, Phoebe and Rachel; Carina and Franc Roddam, Ithaka, Flynn and Sidonie; Sarah and Neil Sutton, William and Emily.

Thank you also to the following companies for lending props:
Blue Lemon, 160 Munster Road, London SW6 5RA. Tel: 020 7610 9464
The Dining Room Shop, 64 White Hart Lane, London, SW13 0PZ. Tel: 020 8878 1020
Cath Kidston, 11 Clarendon Cross, London W11 4AP. Tel: 020 7221 4000
Cologne & Cotton, 791 Fulham Road, London SW6 5HD. Tel: 020 7736 9261
Czech & Speake, 125 Fulham Road, London SW3 6RT. Tel: 020 7225 3667
Joss Graham, 10 Eccleston Street, London SW1W 9LT. Tel: 020 7730 4370. E.mail: joss.graham@ninternet.com (oriental and ethnic textiles, see page 11)
Judy Greenwood Antiques, 657 Fulham Road, London SW6 5PY. Tel: 020 7736 6037
The Lacquer Chest, 75 Kensington Church Street, London W8 4BG. Tel: 020 7938 2070
Lunn Antiques, 86 New Kings Road, London SW6 4LU. Tel: 020 7736 4683
Mini Boden, mail order children's clothes.Tel: 020 8453 1535
Tobias and The Angel, 68 White Hart Lane, London SW13 0PZ. Tel: 020 8878 8902
Architect Brian Ma Siy, pages 5, 20, 21, 30 and 31, contact 020 7978 6431

Collins & Brown would especially like to thank Alison Wormleighton for her invaluable help with the text and Nick Reynolds for design assistance.

Bibliography

Chambers Modern Quotations
The Christopher Robin Book of Verse, A A Milne
Collins Gem Quotations
Graces, June Cotner
The Lion Christian Quotations Collection, compiled by Hannah Ward & Jennifer Wild
Home Sweet Home, compiled by Susan Cuthbert
How Not to Raise a Perfect Child, Libby Purves
Memories with Food at Gipsy House, Felicity & Roald Dahl
The NIV Bible
The Oxford Dictionary of Modern Quotations
The Parent Talk Guide to Childhood Years, Steve Chalke
The Parent Talk Guide to Toddler Years, Steve Chalke
The Pooh Book of Quotations, A A Milne, compiled by Brian Silbey
Quotable Women, Running Press
The Secrets of Joy, Running Press